SCHOLASTIC

AF650314

Mastering Science 5

Name ______________________________

Class ______________________________

Photo attributions and credits:

Speech Bubble: Amada44(http://commons.wikimedia.org/wiki/File:Speech_bubble.svg)
pp.6-18: The following images are from Wikimedia commons: Mayankvagadiya(http://commons.wikimedia.org/wiki/File:Gir_lion-Gir_forest,junagadh,gujarat,india.jpeg), Just chaos(http://commons.wikimedia.org/wiki/File:Striped_Hyena_5.jpg), Janice Harney Carr, Center for Disease Control(http://commons.wikimedia.org/wiki/File:Body_lice.jpg), Ltshears(http://commons.wikimedia.org/wiki/File:Diamondback_Terrapin.jpg), Stefan Laube (Tauchgurke)(http://commons.wikimedia.org/wiki/File:Bradypus.jpg), Sannse(http://commons.wikimedia.org/wiki/File:Ring_tailed_lemur_and_twins.jpg), Koshy Koshy(http://commons.wikimedia.org/wiki/File:Indian_(Collared%3F)_Scops_Owl.jpg), Diliff(http://commons.wikimedia.org/wiki/File:Koala_climbing_tree.jpg), AndrewIves(http://commons.wikimedia.org/wiki/File:Mink1.jpg), Wrtiii3644 at en.wikipedia(http://commons.wikimedia.org/wiki/File:SStringray.jpg), H. Zell(http://commons.wikimedia.org/wiki/File:Acanthurus_leucosternon_01.JPG), User:DustyDingo (http://commons.wikimedia.org/wiki/File:Frog_on_bough.jpg), Kmanoj(http://commons.wikimedia.org/wiki/File:Marsh_Crocodiles_basking_in_the_sun.JPG), J.M.Garg(http://commons.wikimedia.org/wiki/File:House_Sparrow_%28Passer_domesticus%29-_Female_in_Kolkata_I_IMG_3787.jpg), Scott Harrison(http://commons.wikimedia.org/wiki/File:Hippopotamus_amphibius.JPG), Nhobgood Nick Hobgood(http://commons.wikimedia.org/wiki/File:Niphates_callista_%28Tube_sponge%29_with_sea_cucumbers_and_cup_corals.jpg), Matt Wilson/Jay Clark, NOAA NMFS AFSC. (http://commons.wikimedia.org/wiki/File:Fish3532_-_Flickr_-_NOAA_Photo_Library.jpg), ryanoelke(http://upload.wikimedia.org/wikipedia/commons/thumb/2/26/Slate_pencil_sea_urchin.jpg/800px-Slate_pencil_sea_urchin.jpg), D. Davesne(http://commons.wikimedia.org/wiki/File:Heligmosomoides.jpg), Nhobgood(http://commons.wikimedia.org/wiki/File:Squid_komodo.jpg), Copyright © 2006 Steven G. Johnson(http://commons.wikimedia.org/wiki/File:Blue-lobster.jpg), User: Inkub0(http://commons.wikimedia.org/wiki/File:Snail.jpg), Aruna at ml.wikipedia (http://commons.wikimedia.org/wiki/File:Earthworm.JPG), Marina Campos Vinhal(http://commons.wikimedia.org/wiki/File:Yellow_crab.jpg), G.-U. Tolkiehn(http://commons.wikimedia.org/wiki/File:Chorthippus_parallelus_8586.jpg), Marcus334(http://commons.wikimedia.org/wiki/File:MNP_Grey_Languer.JPG), Mohan Raj(http://commons.wikimedia.org/wiki/File:Two-Elephants.JPG), Scott Harrison(http://commons.wikimedia.org/wiki/File:Hippopotamus_amphibius.JPG), Per Harald Olsen(http://commons.wikimedia.org/wiki/File:Svalbardrein_pho.jpg), Yann(http://commons.wikimedia.org/wiki/File:Camels,_Osyam,_Rajasthan,_India.jpg), Photographed by Adrian Pingstone in March 2008(http://commons.wikimedia.org/wiki/File:Sand_cat_at_bristol_zoo_arp.jpg), Marek Szczepanek(http://commons.wikimedia.org/wiki/File:Natrix_natrix_(Marek_Szczepanek).jpg), Nyanatusita(http://commons.wikimedia.org/wiki/File:Hipposideros_lankadiva_Kelaart%27s_leaf-nosed_bat_2.jpg), Baldhur(http://commons.wikimedia.org/wiki/File:Seehunde_auf_Duene.jpg), Andreas Trepte (http://commons.wikimedia.org/wiki/File:Camels,_Osyam,_Rajasthan,_India.jpg), Andreas Trepte (http://commons.wikimedia.org/wiki/File:Great_cormorant_flock.jpg). pp.19-20: The following images are from Wikimedia commons: User : Keith Edkins(http://commons.wikimedia.org/wiki/File:RedRoo.JPG), Diliff(http://commons.wikimedia.org/wiki/File:Koala_climbing_tree.jpg). p.44: The following image is from Wikimedia commons: FDB(http://commons.wikimedia.org/wiki/File:FDBs_madpyramide_2011.jpg). P.51: The following images are from Wikimedia commons: Anetode(http://commons.wikimedia.org/wiki/File:Scorbutic_gums.jpg), Almazi(http://commons.wikimedia.org/wiki/File:Goitre.jpg), James Heilman, MD(http://commons.wikimedia.org/wiki/File:Anemia.JPG). p.57: The following image is from Wikimedia commons: User:Pengo(http://commons.wikimedia.org/wiki/File:Monocot_vs_dicot_Pengo.jpg). p.60: All images are from Fables, except the following which are from Wikimedia commons: Frank Vincentz(http://en.wikipedia.org/wiki/File:Euphorbia_rhizophora2_ies.jpg), CrazyD, 26 October 2005(http://commons.wikimedia.org/wiki/File:Bryophyllum_daigremontianum_nahaufnahme2.jpg). pp.61-63: The following images are from Wikimedia commons: Schnobby(http://commons.wikimedia.org/wiki/File:Fern_Spores.jpg), Caryrivard(http://commons.wikimedia.org/wiki/File:Tube_Grafting_Technique.jpg), Photographer: Anuj Kumar Pradhan [User: File Upload Bot (Eloquence)](http://commons.wikimedia.org/wiki/File:Kalimpong_cacti.jpg), User: Lamiot(http://commons.wikimedia.org/wiki/File:Mangroves1.JPG), High Contrast(http://commons.wikimedia.org/wiki/File:Aquatic_plant_in_the_Tegernsee.JPG). p.69: The following images are from Wikimedia commons: MichaelMaggs(http://commons.wikimedia.org/wiki/File:Coloured,_textured_craft_card.jpg), miya(http://commons.wikimedia.org/wiki/File:Chicken_egg02_binovular.jpg), Copyright © 2004 David Monniaux(http://commons.wikimedia.org/wiki/File:Pain_epices_DSC00141.jpg), Mcnultyc1(http://commons.wikimedia.org/wiki/File:Centering.jpg). pp.75-78: The following images are from Wikimedia commons: Eurico Zimbres FGEL/UERJ(http://commons.wikimedia.org/wiki/File:Granite.jpg), Norbert Nagel, Mörfelden-Walldorf, Germany(http://commons.wikimedia.org/wiki/File:Lanzarote_-_stones_of_a_wall_-_pumice_stone.jpg), User: Locutus Borg(http://commons.wikimedia.org/wiki/File:ObsidianOregon.jpg), B.navez(http://commons.wikimedia.org/wiki/File:Scoria_AmsterdamIsland_2_edit.jpg), Photo by Violet Gottrop.(http://commons.wikimedia.org/wiki/File:LionHeadSandstone.jpg), Lamiot(http://commons.wikimedia.org/wiki/File:LimestonesStonemasonryPierreCalcaireG%C3%A9liveVauban0.jpg), User: Jeanot. Source: US Govt(http://commons.wikimedia.org/wiki/File:ShaleUSGOV.jpg), High Contrast(http://commons.wikimedia.org/wiki/File:Nagelfluh_im_Geologischen_Museum_M%C3%BCnchen.JPG), Rob Lavinsky, iRocks.com – CC-BY-SA-3.0(http://commons.wikimedia.org/wiki/File:Atacamite-Gypsum-mrz349a.jpg), Apphim(http://commons.wikimedia.org/wiki/File:Liquefaction-charbon.jpg), Siim Sepp(http://commons.wikimedia.org/wiki/File:Chlorite_schist.jpg), Huhulenik(http://commons.wikimedia.org/wiki/File:Orthogneiss_Geopark.jpg), LoKiLeCh(http://commons.wikimedia.org/wiki/File:G%C3%B6ttelborn_Th%C3%B6s_Schieferpl%C3%A4ttchen_%281%29.jpg), USGS(http://commons.wikimedia.org/wiki/File:MarbleUSGOV.jpg), User: Tano4595(http://commons.wikimedia.org/wiki/File:Quartzite_2_jpg.jpg). pp.91-92: The following images are from Wikimedia commons: Oguraclutch(http://commons.wikimedia.org/wiki/File:A-1_horseshoe-magnet-red-silver-iron-filings-AHD.jpg), Sofia (next to Alexander Nevsky. p.104: The following images are from Wikimedia commons: Evan-Amos(http://commons.wikimedia.org/wiki/File:Kitchen-Classic-Can-Opener.jpg), User: Horst Frank(http://commons.wikimedia.org/wiki/File:Korkenzieher.jpg), User:Bangin(http://commons.wikimedia.org/wiki/File:Scissor.JPG). p.112: The following images are from Wikimedia commons: Byggxx(http://commons.wikimedia.org/wiki/File:Regenreifen_eines_DTM-Rennwagen.JPG), Mattbuck(http://commons.wikimedia.org/wiki/File:Jubilee_Campus_MMB_Q9_Atrium.jpg). pp.125-126: The following images are from Wikimedia commons: Justin1569 at en.wikipedia(http://commons.wikimedia.org/wiki/File:F5_tornado_Elie_Manitoba_2007.jpg), Astronaut photograph ISS008-E-19646 was taken March 7, 2004, with a Kodak DCS760 digital camera equipped with an 50-mm lens, and is provided by the Earth Observations Laboratory, Johnson Space Center(http://commons.wikimedia.org/wiki/File:Cyclone_Catarina_from_the_ISS_on_March_26_2004.JPG).

This edition specially created for Scholastic India.

First edition 2012
Reprinted 2012, 2013, 2014 (thrice), 2015, 2016, 2018, 2019 2020, 2021, 2022, 2023, 2024, 2025

ISBN 978-81-8477-929-5

Contents

 ISBN 978-81-8477-929-5

Introduction

Mastering Science is an exciting science series for levels 1 to 8. The books have been designed to fulfill the requirements of the National Curriculum Framework (NCF), which has been adopted by CBSE, ICSE and major State Educational Boards.

The series adopts a learner-centred approach, encouraging students to make connections between their role in their immediate environment and the world around them. The coursebooks are filled with lots of colourful photographs and illustrations that expose students to real-life everyday experiences from around the world.

In addition, the series prepares students to meet the challenges of the future by

- following pyramidal pedagogy
- encouraging exploration and innovation
- facilitating observation and logical analysis to support conclusions
- promoting independent learning

Learn More provides activities that hone the students' ability to absorb, infer, classify, experiment and predict.

Explore encourages students to analyse and question.

Learn More

Go for a nature walk around the garden or park. List all the things you hear, see, feel and smell.

I hear	I see	I feel	I smell

Explore

Observe the way in which popcorn is made. Yes No

Can you hear the kernels pop?

Can you smell the popcorn?

Can you see the popcorn?

Did you taste the popcorn?

KEEPING HEALTHY

To be strong and fit, we must eat healthy food, drink clean water and keep our homes, school and surroundings clean.

14

I Care provides value education in levels 1 to 3.

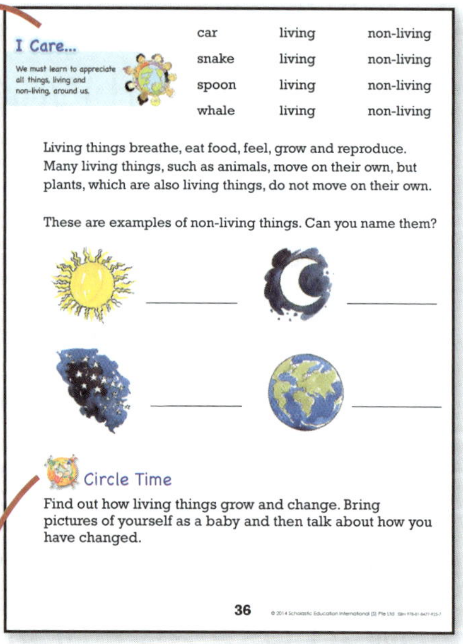

I Care...

We must learn to appreciate all things, living and non-living, around us.

car	living	non-living
snake	living	non-living
spoon	living	non-living
whale	living	non-living

Living things breathe, eat food, feel, grow and reproduce. Many living things, such as animals, move on their own, but plants, which are also living things, do not move on their own.

These are examples of non-living things. Can you name them?

Circle Time

Find out how living things grow and change. Bring pictures of yourself as a baby and then talk about how you have changed.

36

Circle Time promotes exchange of ideas and techniques while laying emphasis on working as a team.

 ISBN 978-81-8477-929-5

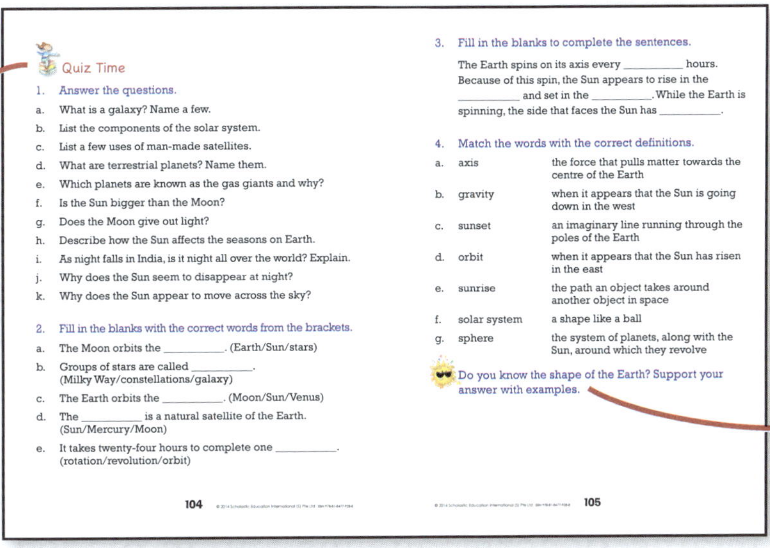

3. Fill in the blanks to complete the sentences.

The Earth spins on its axis every _________ hours. Because of this spin, the Sun appears to rise in the _________ and set in the _________. While the Earth is spinning, the side that faces the Sun has _________.

4. Match the words with the correct definitions.

a.	axis	the force that pulls matter towards the centre of the Earth
b.	gravity	when it appears that the Sun is going down in the west
c.	sunset	an imaginary line running through the poles of the Earth
d.	orbit	when it appears that the Sun has risen in the east
e.	sunrise	the path an object takes around another object in space
f.	solar system	a shape like a ball
g.	sphere	the system of planets, along with the Sun, around which they revolve

Do you know the shape of the Earth? Support your answer with examples.

105

Quiz Time tests knowledge retention and serves as a quick recap of the lesson.

Higher Order Thinking Skills (**HOTS**) questions are included in levels 4 and above. These questions sharpen the students' skills of making inferences, understanding the logic behind a concept and thinking outside the box.

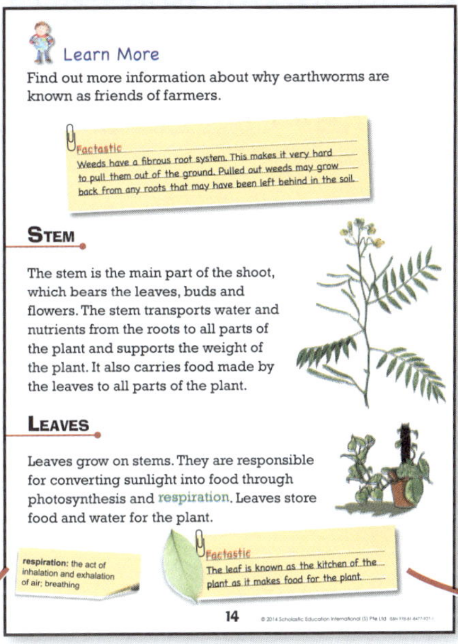

Learn More

Find out more information about why earthworms are known as friends of farmers.

Factastic

Weeds have a fibrous root system. This makes it very hard to pull them out of the ground. Pulled out weeds may grow back from any roots that may have been left behind in the soil.

STEM

The stem is the main part of the shoot, which bears the leaves, buds and flowers. The stem transports water and nutrients from the roots to all parts of the plant and supports the weight of the plant. It also carries food made by the leaves to all parts of the plant.

LEAVES

Leaves grow on stems. They are responsible for converting sunlight into food through photosynthesis and respiration. Leaves store food and water for the plant.

respiration: the act of inhalation and exhalation of air; breathing

Factastic

The leaf is known as the kitchen of the plant as it makes food for the plant.

14

New and difficult words are defined in the **glossary.**

Factastic imparts interesting information and facts related to the topic under discussion.

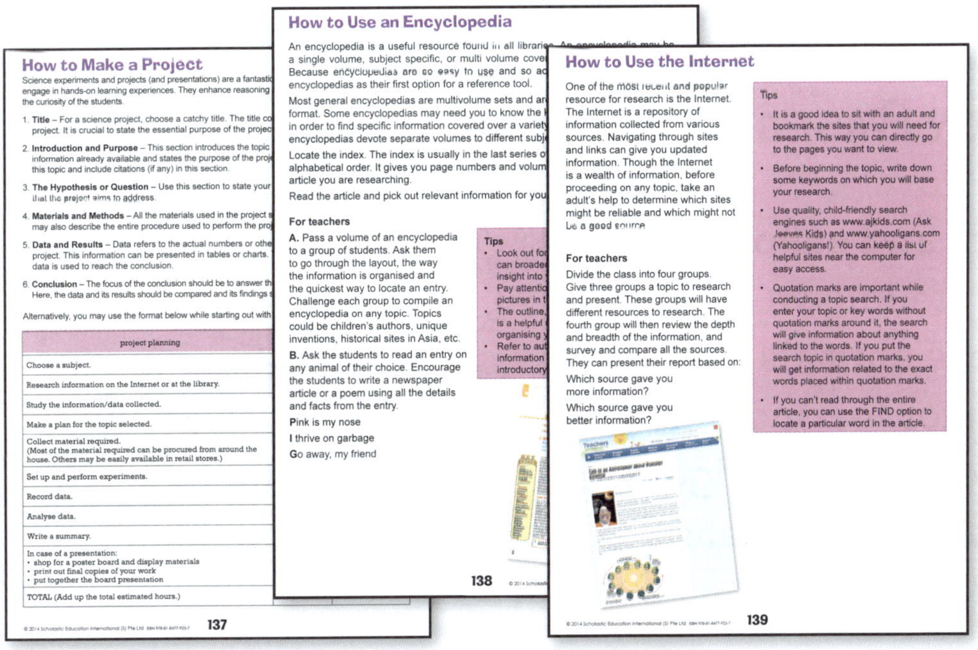

How to Make a Project

How to Use an Encyclopedia

How to Use the Internet

137

138

139

Students are taught to use an atlas, the encyclopedia and the Internet in levels 3 to 5 to do basic research, individually and in groups, to present reports and projects. These help build the ability to learn independently.

 ISBN 978-81 8477-929-5

1
Animals

Animals are found everywhere on Earth. They may be found in forests, mountains, deserts, oceans and in places of human habitation. Animals are vastly different in their appearance, size, habits and features. They can be classified in various ways.

Classification of the Animal Kingdom

The animal kingdom can be classified on the basis of:

- Diet
- Habitat
- Body temperature
- Hours of activity
- Presence or absence of a backbone

Classification Based on Diet

Animals that hunt and eat other animals as food are known as **carnivores**. These animals have long sharp teeth for tearing and ripping flesh. Lions, sharks, tigers, alligators, snakes and cheetahs are examples of carnivores.

lions

 ISBN 978-81-8477-929-5

Herbivores primarily eat plants as food.

Animals that eat both plants as well as animals are known as **omnivores**. Human beings, fish, pigs and bears are examples of omnivores.

Herbivores or omnivores can also be **frugivorous animals**, where fruit constitutes most of their diet.

A **scavenger** feeds on dead animals or remains of animals killed by other animals. Many scavengers have strong jaws or hooked beaks to tear out meat from dead animals. Hyenas and vultures are examples of scavengers.

hyena

Parasites live in or on other organisms. They are dependent on their host for their life functions—to live, grow and multiply. Parasites derive nutrition by sucking food and nutrients from the host's body. Tapeworms and lice are examples of parasites.

lice

Classification Based on Habitat

This classification groups animals according to where they live.

Aquatic animals spend their entire life cycle in water. Most aquatic animals breathe with the help of gills, but whales and dolphins breathe through lungs. Fish, ducks and turtles are some examples of aquatic animals.

turtle

Terrestrial animals live on land. Most terrestrial animals breathe with the help of lungs. Lions, tigers, giraffes, cats and kangaroos are some examples of terrestrial animals.

 ISBN 978-81-8477-929-5

Amphibians live in water as well as on land. Many amphibians begin life with gills and tails, which develop into lungs and legs over time. They are cold-blooded and adjust their body temperature according to their environment. Frogs, toads, salamanders and newts are examples of amphibians.

tree sloth

lemur

Arboreal animals spend most or all of their time on trees. Koalas, lemurs, flying squirrels, tree sloths, spider monkeys and chameleons are examples of arboreal animals. Arboreal animals may have flexible bodies, clawed or sticky feet and prehensile tails to help them adapt to life on trees.

Aerial animals spend much time in air, mostly in flight. They have hollow bones that make them light. Their bodies are aerodynamic in shape.

Classification Based on Body Temperature

Cold-blooded animals take on the temperature of their surroundings. They cannot regulate their own body temperature. They are hot when the surroundings are hot and cold when the surroundings are cold. Reptiles, amphibians and fish are cold-blooded animals. Cold-blooded animals are more active in warm surroundings.

prehensile: adapted for seizing, grasping, or taking hold of something

 ISBN 978-81-8477-929-5

Warm-blooded animals are able to maintain a constant body temperature by producing heat when they are in cool surroundings and by cooling themselves when they are in warm surroundings.

In warm surroundings, some warm-blooded animals sweat or pant to lose heat and stay cool. Humans, apes and monkeys have sweat glands all over their bodies.

To adapt to cold surroundings, many mammals have hair, fur or blubber to help them keep warm. Some warm-blooded animals shiver to produce more heat.

Classification Based on Hours of Activity

Animals can be classified according to the time of day they are active. Most mammals and birds are active during the day and inactive during the night. Such animals are called **diurnal animals**.

owl

koala

Nocturnal animals sleep during the day. They have enhanced night vision, which makes it possible for them to be active during the night. Owls, koalas and bats are nocturnal animals.

Crepuscular animals hunt and stay awake during the cooler hours of the day. These animals are most active at dawn and dusk. The flying squirrel, mink, rabbits and cats are crepuscular animals.

mink

 ISBN 978-81-8477-929-5

Classification Based on the Presence or Absence of a Backbone

Animals with backbones are known as **vertebrates**. They have an internal skeletal system made of bones. These animals include primates such as monkeys and humans, amphibians, reptiles, birds and fish.

Vertebrates have a skin covering that protects their organs. They breathe with lungs or gills. They move with fins or legs. Vertebrates also have heads with brains that are part of a nervous system. They have sense organs such as eyes and nose.

Factastic

About 95% of fishes have skeletons made of bones. These bony fishes have a swim bladder (a gas-filled sac) that can be inflated or deflated, allowing them to float in the water even when not swimming. Fishes which have skeletons made of cartilage do not have a swim bladder. They must swim constantly to keep afloat.

Learn More

Look at the animal's skeleton in the picture.

Observe the size and position of its eye sockets. (It has very good vision.)

Note the long slender legs. (It moves at high speed.)

Which animal's skeleton is it?

____

Compare the skeleton of this animal with a human skeleton. What are the similarities and differences?

 ISBN 978-81-8477-929-5

Characteristics of Vertebrates

name	body structure	reproduction	habitat
Fishes  powder blue tang	• Streamline bodies • Skeletal system is made of either bone or cartilage	Lay eggs	• Live in water and use fins to swim • Breathe with the help of gills
Amphibians  frog	• Cold-blooded • In cold climates, amphibians hibernate during the winter months	Lay eggs	• Live in water and on land • Breathe with the help of gills, lungs, the lining of the mouth or a combination of these
Reptiles  crocodile	• Cold-blooded	Lay eggs	• Mostly live on land and have scaly skin • Most reptiles breathe through lungs • Some reptiles absorb oxygen in water through a membrane in their mouth

 ISBN 978-81-8477-929-5

name	body-structure	reproduction	habitat
Birds  Indian sparrow	• Warm-blooded • Adapted their vertebrate skeleton for flight • Bones and skull are very thin, making their bodies extremely light	Lay eggs	• Birds are the only animals that have feathers • All birds have wings, however, only some can fly
Mammals  hippopotamus	• Warm-blooded	Give birth to fully formed babies and female mammals produce milk to feed their young	• Live on land or in water • Their bodies are covered with hair or fur

Animals that do not have a backbone are known as **invertebrates**. Insects, worms, snails and spiders are invertebrates.

Sponges have tube-like bodies. They live in water. Sponges do not move from place to place. They usually attach themselves to rocks. They filter tiny organisms out of the water for food.

tube sponge

 ISBN 978-81-8477-929-5

jellyfish

Coelenterates have tube or sac-like bodies. They have mouth openings surrounded by tentacles. Jellyfish, corals and sea anemones are examples of coelenterates.

sea urchin

Echinoderms have external skeletons made of limbs. Their bodies are arranged in five parts or in multiples of five. They live in seawater. Starfish, sea urchins and sea cucumbers are examples of echinoderms.

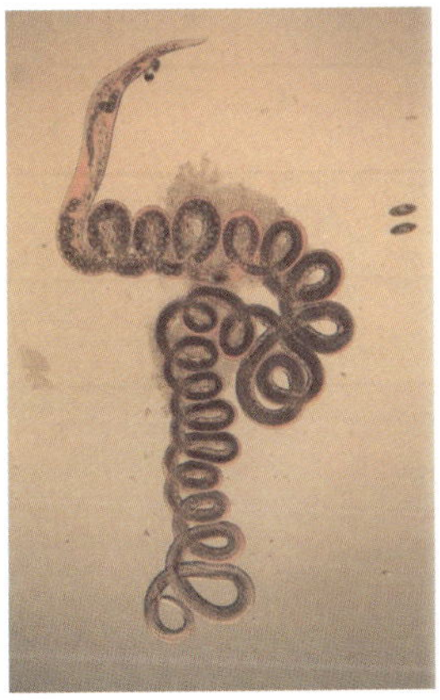
worms

Worms live in different habitats. Some have flat bodies with a head and a simple nervous system. Others have smooth round bodies. Some worms have body parts called segments. Flatworms, roundworms, earthworms, hookworms and rotifers are examples of worms.

squid

Mollusks have soft bodies enclosed in hard shells. Snails, slugs, octopus, squid, mussels, oysters, clams, scallops and cuttlefish are examples of mollusks.

blue lobster

Arthropods have segmented bodies and a hard external skeleton called exoskeleton. Arthropods include insects, arachnids (spiders), centipedes, millipedes and crustaceans such as crabs, lobsters and shrimp.

 ISBN 978-81-8477-929-5

Learn More

Identify each of these creatures and say how their body is supported.

 ISBN 978-81-8477-929-5

Animal Adaptation

The clothes we wear, the food we eat and sometimes even our physical features change depending on the environment. Just as humans adapt to their living conditions, animals also adapt to their environment in order to survive.

Adaptations are characteristics that birds and animals have developed over the years which help them survive in their environment or habitat.

In dense forests, animals rely on scent and sound signals for their safety. They use alarm calls or territorial calls. Animals use stripes, spots or other patterns on their bodies to camouflage themselves in the thick foliage.

Some animals use their long limbs (including their tail, as a fifth limb) to move from one tree to another. They use their sharp claws for holding on to the branches of tall trees.

A monkey uses its tail like a fifth limb. Monkeys can leap up to 30 feet, as they move from one tree to another. They can use their tails for gripping the branches of trees.

The fastest animal on land, the cheetah, has strong, powerful legs and a streamlined body that help it to run fast. It also has a wide nasal passage and a flat ribcage that allows for the quick intake of air while running.

An elephant has a long trunk. Its trunk is actually a blend of the upper lip and the nose. The elephant uses

 ISBN 978-81-8477-929-5

its trunk just as human beings use their hands. The trunk is used for drinking water, bringing food to the mouth as well as for picking small objects.

The hippopotamus lives in swampy areas. It has a lot of fat under its skin, which helps it to stay afloat. Its eyes, nostrils and ears are on the top of its head because most of its body stays immersed in water and only the head remains above water. This makes it easy for the hippopotamus to see, hear and breathe while hiding in water.

The reindeer has wide hooves that prevent it from sinking in the snow. They have thick fur to keep them dry and warm in cold regions.

Factastic

Many lizards shed their tails to escape predators. Some lizards can change their colour to blend into the environment. This camouflage protects them from predators.

Learn More

Use an encyclopedia to find out how the polar bear has adapted to the polar environment.

 ISBN 978-81-8477-929-5

Camels have wide feet that keep them from sinking in the sand. They have long eyelashes that prevent the sand from getting in their eyes. They can also close their nostrils which prevents the sand from getting in. Their light-coloured skin helps them camouflage in the sand.

Sand cats have thick fur on their feet that keeps them from sinking in the sand. They are nocturnal animals. They live in burrows during the day and hunt at night. They meet their water requirement from the food they eat.

A snake is equipped with fangs. A fang is a tooth that is adapted to work like a syringe. Snakes use their fangs to inject venom into their prey as they hunt.

Bats are nocturnal mammals that have very poor vision. They emit high-pitched sounds and listen to resultant echoes to locate their prey and nearby objects. This process is known as **echolocation**. Bats have wings that help them glide. Their strong claws help them hang upside down.

 ISBN 978-81-8477-929-5

Birds have adapted their vertebrate skeleton for flight. Their bones and skulls are very thin, making their bodies extremely light and aerodynamic in shape. Just as we use our legs to move about, birds use wings to fly and glide as they go from one place to another.

Seals have adapted to live on land, in water as well as on ice. They have a streamlined body, which helps them propel themselves in water. They have short hindlimbs, known as flippers. The flippers help them to swim. They have a lot of blood in their body, which stores enough oxygen for them to dive in deep waters and survive for about twenty to thirty minutes without breathing.

Animals do different things to survive in the cold winter months. Some animals and birds migrate, or travel to regions of warmer climate in search of food and shelter.

Birds fly a very long distance as they migrate during the autumn and winter months to warmer regions. Whales migrate in search of food during the winter. Some fish may swim south, or move to deeper, warmer waters. Some animals, such as the earthworm, go down deeper into the soil to escape the cold.

aerodynamic: the branch of mechanics that deals with the motion of air and other gases and with the effects of such motion on bodies in the medium.

 ISBN 978-81-8477-929-5

Explore

Write the reasons and uses of the animal adaptations. The first one has been done for you.

animal feature	does this help the animal live in a hot or cold environment?	how does this feature help the animal cope with the environment?
long eyelashes	hot	to keep the sand and wind out of a camel's eyes
small ears		
long tail		
feet with separate toes		
big ears		
furry coat		
thick feathers		
huddling together with other animals		
burying itself		
hibernating		
storing food		
thick layer of fat		
long trunk		

 ISBN 978-81-8477-929-5

Primates are mammals with large brains and complex well-developed hands and feet, complete with fingers and toes. They include monkeys, chimpanzees, gorillas and humans.

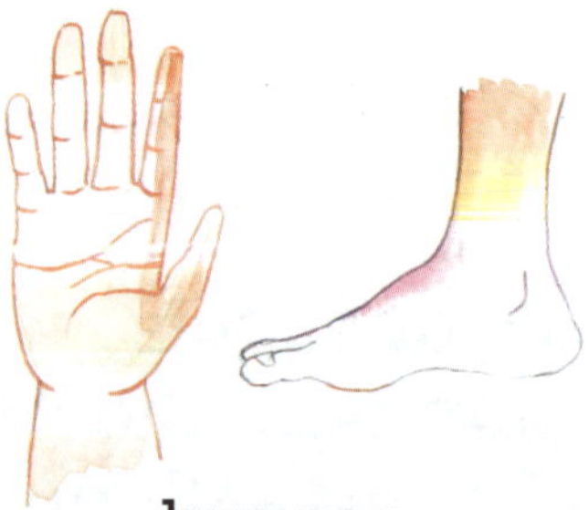

humans

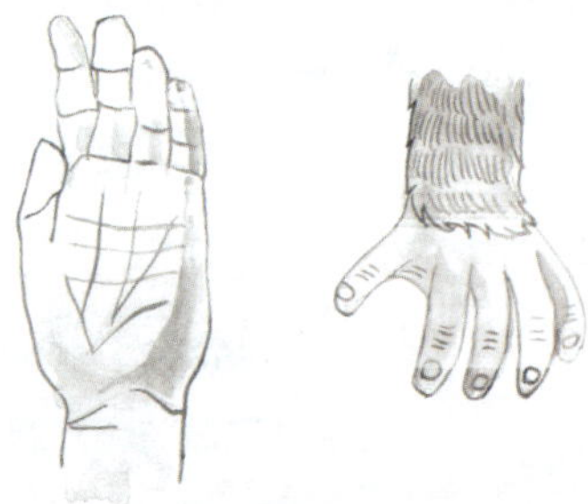

gorilla

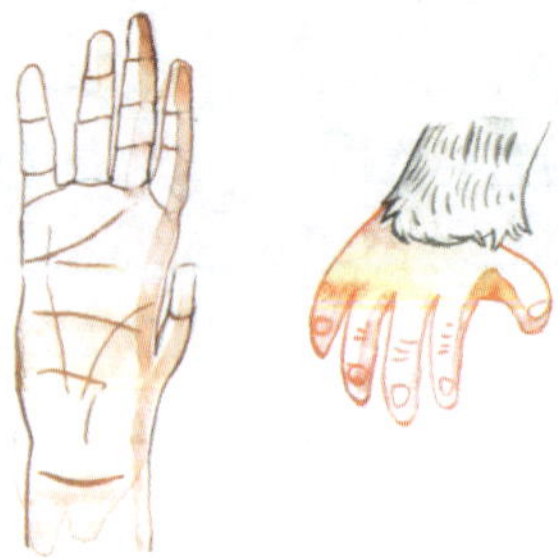

chimpanzee

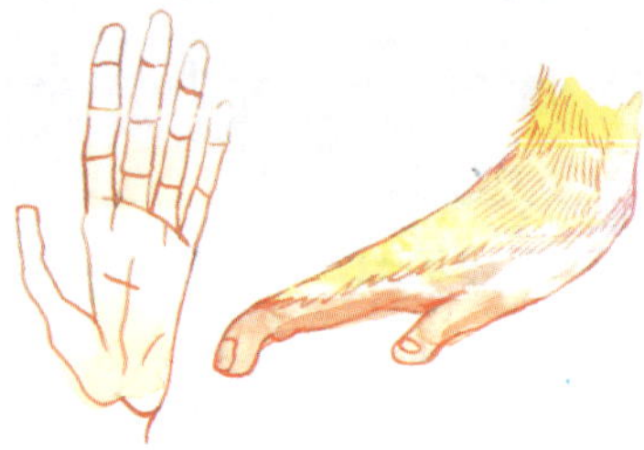

monkey

They have a highly developed sense of colour. Primates have developed language and communication skills. They have eyes in front of their heads, allowing them to judge depth and distance. Monkeys and apes walk on all four limbs. Humans are the only primates that walk on two legs. Primates give birth to fully formed offspring after a long gestation period in the mother's womb.

Marsupials are members of the mammal family. They have an abdominal pouch to carry their young ones. At birth the babies are not fully developed. They develop later in the pouch or the marsupium. A baby kangaroo lives in its mother's pouch for about six months.

 ISBN 978-81-8477-929-5

Factastic

Unlike the kangaroos that have pouches that open upwards, towards their heads, koalas have pouches that are back-facing, that is, they open towards their hind legs.

Explore

Most mammals walk on four legs. Only humans walk upright on two legs. Mammals that live in water have flippers, or fins, for swimming. Mammals include primates, such as humans and monkeys, marsupials, rodents, whales, dolphins and seals. Find out more information about primates and how human beings evolved from them.

Circle Time

The environment and all living beings within that environment are interdependent. Together they form the ecosystem, which is a combination of living as well as non-living things that coexist in that habitat. The Earth is an example of an ecosystem, as is a small garden or even a potted plant.

Discuss which living and non-living things interact with each other in these ecosystems.

 ISBN 978-81-8477-929-5

Endangered Species

There are several species of animals that are now facing extinction. These are regarded as endangered species. With a little awareness we can save them from becoming extinct. It is very important to save the endangered species because the ecosystem they live in is also threatened by their extinction. For example, the rhinoceros is now an endangered species, as it is indiscriminately hunted for its horns. Rhinos eat various plants and help in the dispersal of their seeds. Their dung enhances the fertility of the soil. Without the rhinoceros, its ecosystem also faces extinction.

Quiz Time

1. Answer the questions.

a. What are the differences between mammals, amphibians and reptiles?

b. What is the meaning of the word 'adaptation'?

c. What are primates? Give five examples of primates. List five distinctive features of primates.

d. What are marsupials? Give two examples of marsupials.

e. What is migration? Explain in fifty words.

f. Explain how animals are classified on the basis of body temperature.

g. How are scavengers different from parasites?

h. List any five features of vertebrates.

i. Explain two reasons why animals adapt to their habitats.

 ISBN 978-81-8477-929-5

2. Find and circle the words from the box in the word grid.

omnivores nocturnal diurnal scavengers
terrestrial vertebrates mammals marsupials
primates amphibians

w	s	c	a	v	e	n	g	e	r	s	o
s	o	j	g	c	x	x	y	x	n	u	i
a	m	p	h	i	b	i	a	n	s	u	o
f	n	o	c	t	u	r	n	a	l	m	k
d	i	u	r	n	a	l	e	b	u	a	m
g	v	g	g	f	d	s	r	v	p	m	n
f	o	p	r	i	m	a	t	e	s	m	h
d	r	g	j	i	y	d	z	x	l	a	g
t	e	r	r	e	s	t	r	i	a	l	f
i	s	g	s	d	n	m	s	e	a	s	f
v	e	r	t	e	b	r	a	t	e	s	d
u	j	m	a	r	s	u	p	i	a	l	s

 ISBN 978-81-8477-929-5

3. Fill in the blanks with the correct words from the brackets.

a. Animals that swim in water have ____________ bodies. (thin/streamlined/stout)

b. ___________________ have soft bodies enclosed in hard shells. (Reptiles/Anthropods/Mollusks)

c. In hot surroundings, some warm-blooded animals sweat or pant to lose ____________. (fat/heat/sweat)

4. Indicate whether the following statements are true (T) or false (F).

a. Most herbivores have flat teeth for grinding and chewing plants. ☐

b. Most diurnal animals burrow and sleep during the day and hunt at night. ☐

c. Aerial animals have heavy bones. ☐

What is the importance of opposable thumbs in primates?

 ISBN 978-81-8477-929-5

2
The Skeletal System

Various systems in our body control the vital organs and help them run smoothly. The nervous system controls all the other body systems. The digestive system helps humans turn the food they eat into energy. The respiratory system helps humans breathe. The muscular system allows us to move. The circulatory system supplies blood to all parts of the body.

Skeletal System

The skeletal system provides shape and form to the body. It also protects the body and allows movement.

The skeletal system is made up of bones. There are 206 bones in an adult human body, to which softer tissues and other organs of the body are attached.

The vital organs of the body are protected by the skeletal system.

Factastic

The term 'skeleton' comes from a Greek word which means 'dried up'.

ISBN 978-81-8477-929-5

BONES

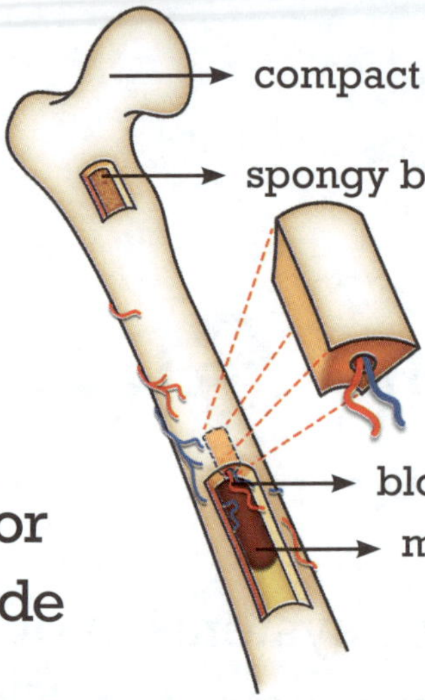

Bones are made up of tissues which are dense. Bone tissue is made up of bone cells. Bone cells, along with the minerals stored in the bones, give the bones their strength and a certain amount of flexibility. Compact bone is the hard, protective exterior seen in all bones. Spongy bone is found inside the compact bone and is very porous.

There are four kinds of bones in the human body.

Long bones: The bones of the forelimbs and the hindlimbs belong to this category such as tibia, femur, ulna and radius.

Short bones: These are cube-shaped and are found in the wrists (carpals) as well as the ankles (tarsals).

Flat bones: These are broad, have muscles attached to them and they protect the organs. The cranial bones are an example of flat bones.

Irregular bones: All other bones are known as irregular bones. The bones of the vertebrae are categorised as irregular bones.

Factastic

About 2.6 million red blood cells are produced per second by the bone marrow. These new blood cells substitute those that are worn out. Minerals, such as calcium and phosphorus, are stored in the bones. Blood cells are produced by the marrow located in some bones.

porous: full of pores, holes

 ISBN 978-81-8477-929-5

Skull

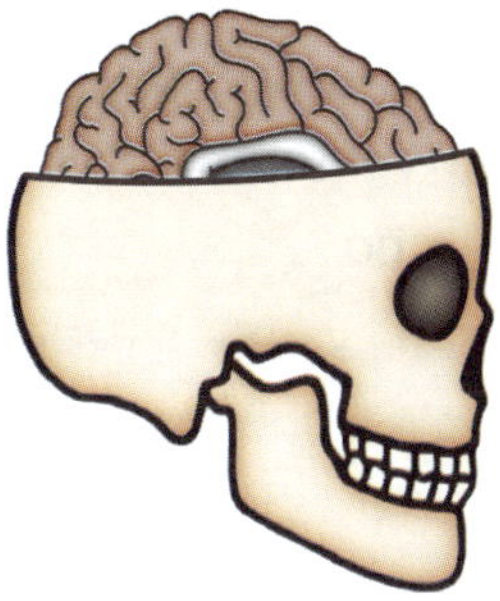

The skull is made up of 29 bones. At the top of the skull is the **cranium**. It protects the brain. The cranium is made up of eight **cranial bones** that fit together tightly. In the front of the skull there are 14 facial bones that form the shape of the face. The upper jaw has two large bones called **maxillary bones** that are joined together. The lower jawbone is the only bone in the skull that can move. It opens and closes to help us talk and chew food. The jawbone holds the teeth in place.

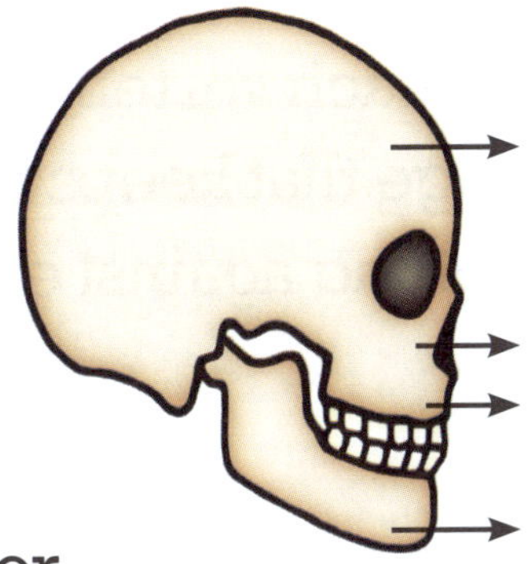

Vertebral column

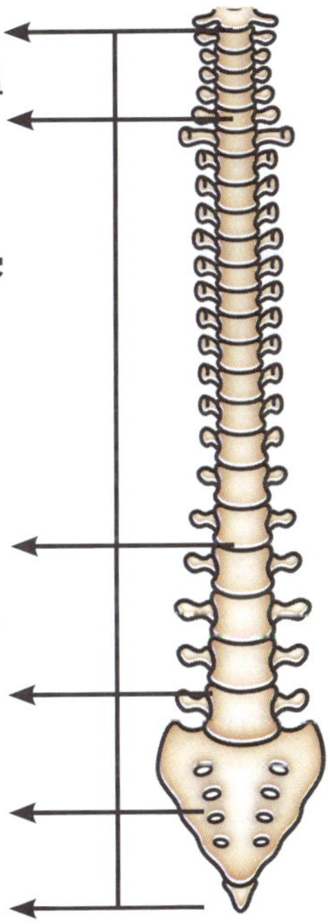

The vertebral column, also known as the **spinal column** or **backbone**, consists of thirty-three irregular shaped bones, known as the vertebrae. The vertebral column is divided into five parts. The first seven vertebrae at the top are called the **cervical vertebrae**. These bones are in the back of the neck, just below the brain. They support the head and neck. The **thoracic vertebrae** are located below the cervical vertebrae. They anchor the ribs in place. The **lumbar vertebrae** lie below the thoracic vertebrae. Below the lumbar vertebrae is the **sacrum**. It is made up of five vertebrae. At the bottom of the spine is the **coccyx**, a bone made of four **fused vertebrae**. They help hold the body's weight and keep its balance.

The backbone protects the spinal cord, which controls most of our bodily functions. It also allows us to stand upright as well

 ISBN 978-81-8477-929-5

as maintain our balance. In between each vertebra is a layer of cartilage that keeps the bones from rubbing against each other.

> **Factastic**
> The atlas (the first cervical vertebra) allows the head to nod yes and the axis (the second cervical vertebra) allows the head to shake no.

Learn More

Find out how the structure and functions of the human respiratory, digestive, circulatory, skeletal, muscular and nervous systems are interconnected.

Ribcage

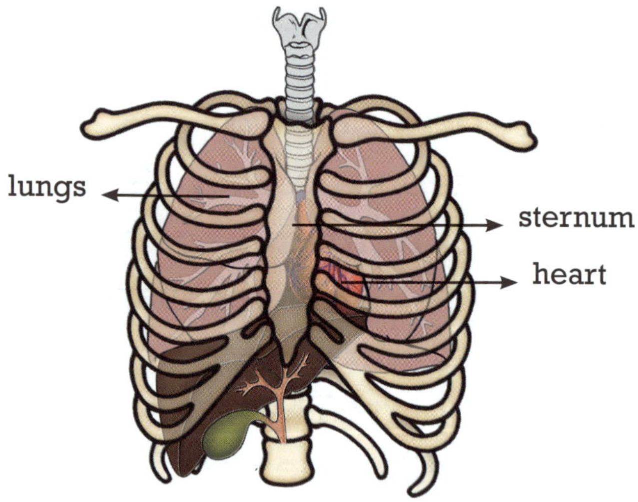

The ribcage is a cage of bones in the trunk of the body. The ribs are flat, thin bones that curve to form a protective cage around the organs in the upper body. The ribcage is made up of twelve pairs of bones. The first seven pairs of ribs are attached in the front to the **sternum**, a strong bone in the centre of the chest. The ribs protect the heart, lungs, stomach, kidneys and spleen.

Explore

Inhale deeply and exhale slowly. Observe as we inhale, the muscle between the ribcage lifts it up. This lift allows the lungs to expand. As we release our breath and exhale, the ribcage goes down and air is released from the lungs.

  ISBN 978-81-8477-929-5

Limbs

The human body has two pairs of limbs.

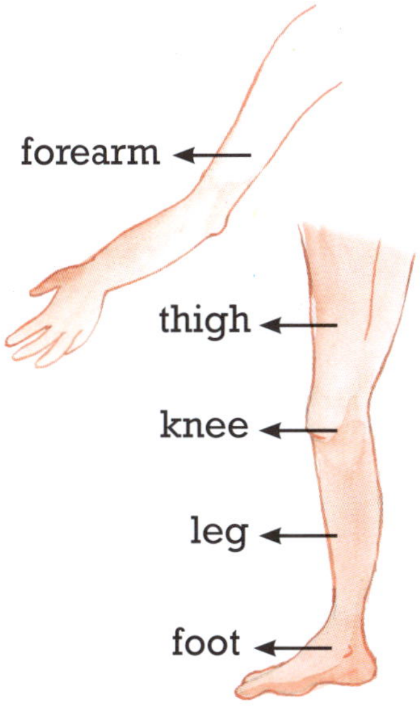

- The upper extremity or the forelimb consists of the arm and the hand.
- The lower extremity or the hind limb consists of the thigh, the leg, the foot and the kneecap (or patella).

The upper limbs are the arms. Each arm is attached to a shoulder blade. The arm is made up of three bones—the **humerus** which is above the elbow, and the **radius** and **ulna** which are below the elbow.

At the end of the radius and ulna are eight smaller bones that make up the wrist. The hand is made up of five bones. Each finger on the hand has three bones, except for the thumb, which has two. Together the bones of the arms help grasp and pick up things. They also help throw, push, pull and write.

The lower limbs are the legs. They are attached to a circular group of bones called the pelvis. The **pelvis** is made up of the two large hip bones. The leg bones are strong to help support the body's weight. The bone that goes from the pelvis to the knee is called the **femur**. It is the longest bone in the body. At the knee, there's a triangular shaped bone called the **patella** that protects the knee joint. Below the knee are two other leg bones, **tibia** and **fibula**.

At the ankle, the lower leg bones connect to a large bone in the foot called **talus**. Next to the talus are six other bones. The foot has five bones. Each toe has three tiny bones, except the big toe, which has two. The leg bones help the body stand and walk. They also help balance the body and keep it upright.

 ISBN 978-81-8477-929-5

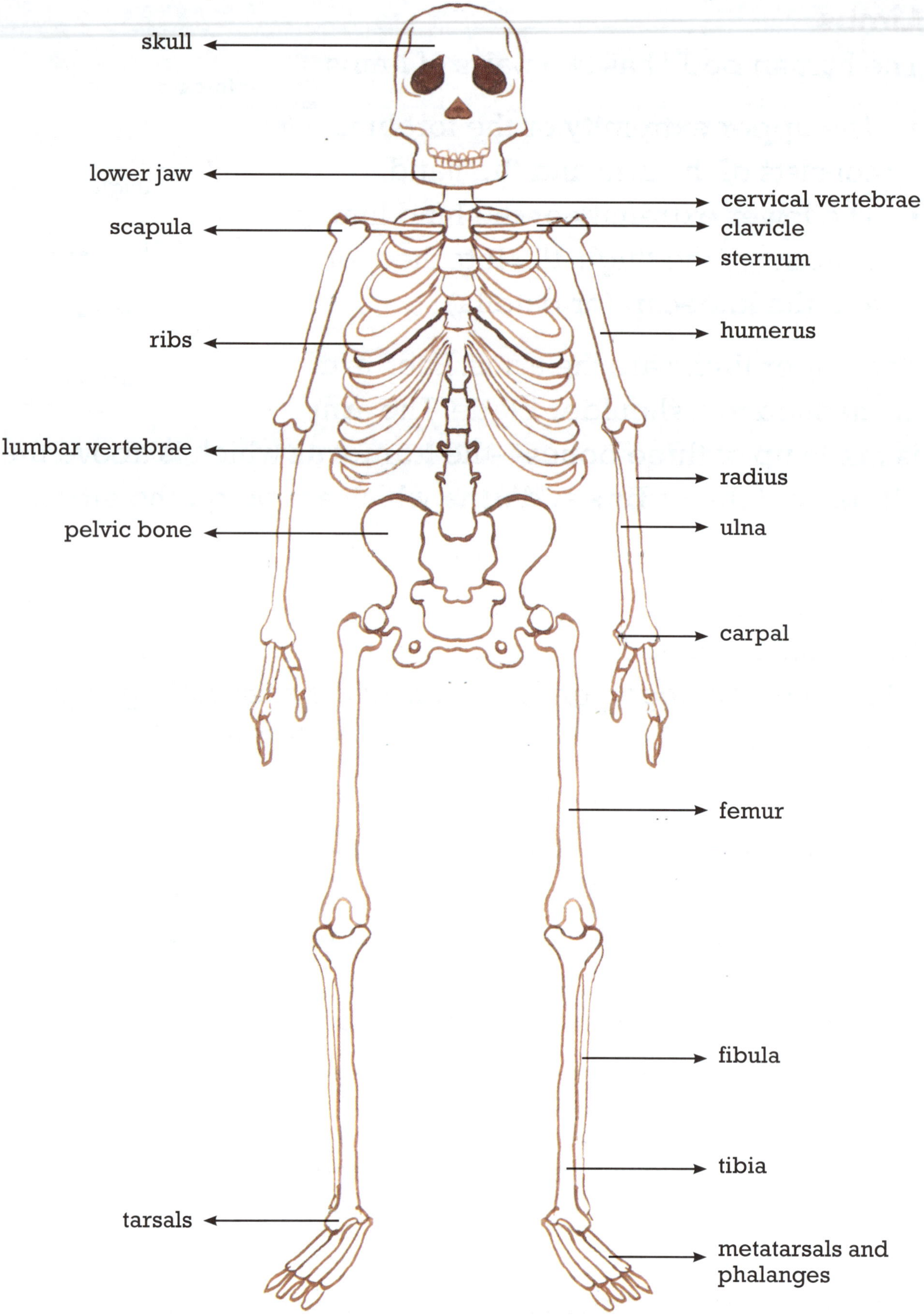

 ISBN 978-81-8477-929-5

Muscles and Movement

Muscles are parts of the body that help in movement. The movements of the body are carried out as a result of the interaction between the muscles and the skeletal system. **Tendons** are long, flexible cables that connect muscles to the bones; while **ligaments** connect two or more bones together. The **cartilage** is a tough, elastic like substance that holds the bones in place at joints. Without the protective cartilage, the bones would rub against each other and wear out.

Feel your muscles when

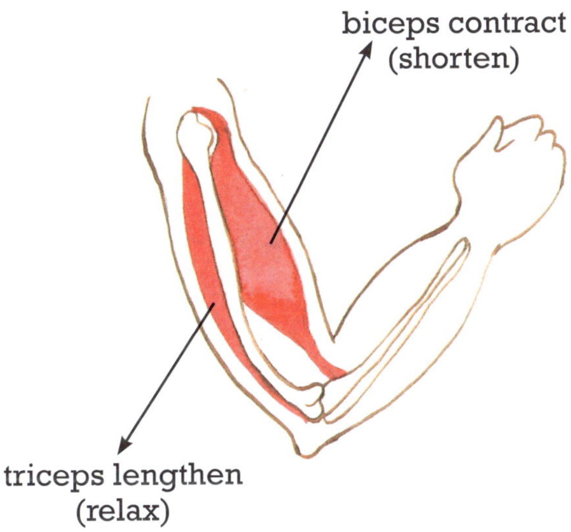

you bend your arm.

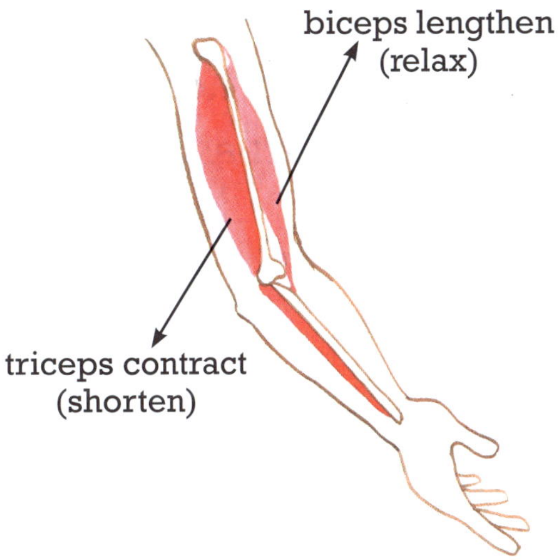

you make your arm straight.

The biceps in the front of the upper arm is a **flexor**. The triceps at the back of the upper arm is an **extensor**. When we bend at the elbow, the biceps contract. Then the biceps relax and the triceps contract to straighten the elbow.

There are three kinds of muscles in the human body—skeletal, smooth and cardiac muscles.

Skeletal muscles are attached to bones in the legs, arms, abdomen, chest and neck. They hold the skeleton together,

 ISBN 978-81-8477-929-5

give the body shape and help it move. They are also called **voluntary muscles**. Their movement is controlled by the brain. They can contract quickly.

Smooth muscles are found in the walls of the stomach, intestines and the blood vessels. They help move food through the digestive system. They help blood move along blood vessels and maintain blood pressure. Smooth muscles take longer to contract than skeletal muscles. They are also called **involuntary muscles**. They are automatically controlled by the nervous system.

Cardiac muscles are found in the heart. They are also involuntary muscles. Their regular, strong contractions force blood out of the heart as it beats.

Explore

Imagine the springs are your muscles. What happens to them when the wooden arm is raised and lowered?

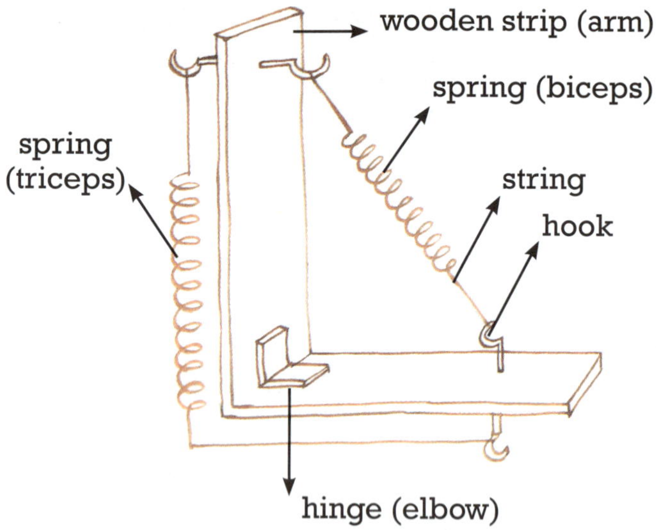

JOINTS

The point at which two or more bones meet is called a joint. They allow our bodies to move in different ways. Some joints, such as knees and elbows, open and close like hinges. While the shoulder or hip joint move backward, forward, and sideways or have rotating movements.

 ISBN 978-81-8477-929-5

Joints are categorised by their range of movement. **Immovable**, or **fibrous joints** don't allow movement. For example, the skull is made of immovable bony plates. Partially movable joints allow little movement. They are linked by cartilage. For example, each of the vertebrae in the spine moves in accordance to the one above and below it. This coordinated movement gives the spine its flexibility. Freely **movable joints** move in different directions such as the hip, shoulders, elbows, knees, wrists and ankles.

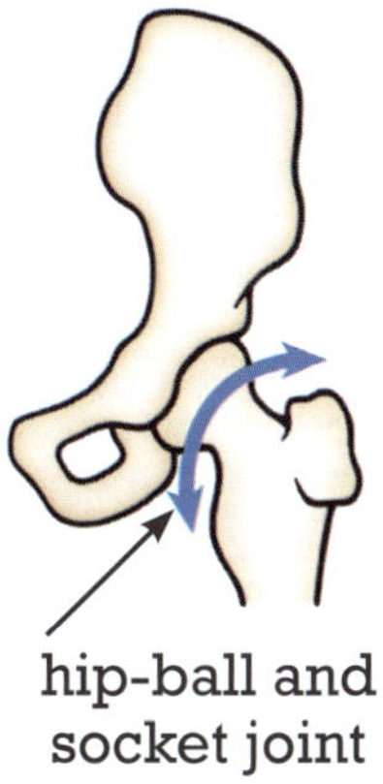

Ball and socket joints allow movements in all directions. The hip and the shoulder are examples of ball and socket joints.

Hinged joints allow movement in one direction. They include joints in the fingers, toes, elbows and knees. Like hinges on a door which allow it to open one way, hinge joints bend the arms and legs in one direction.

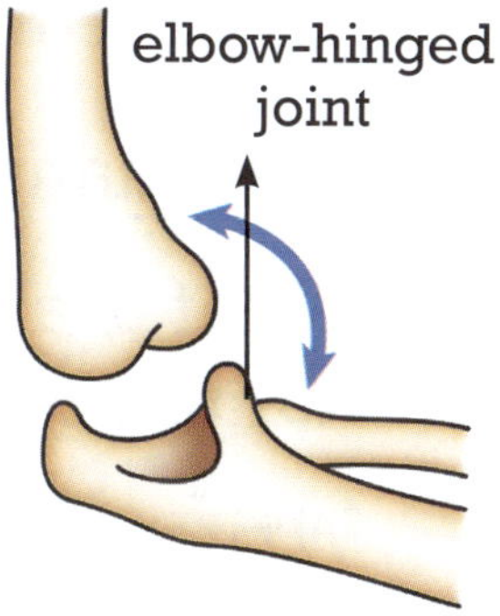

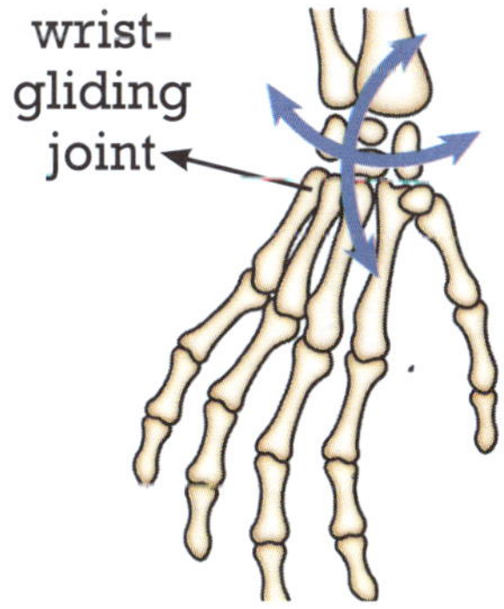

Gliding joints are composed of several interconnected bones with many joint surfaces. They allow sideways movements as well as movement in one direction. The wrist and ankle have gliding joints.

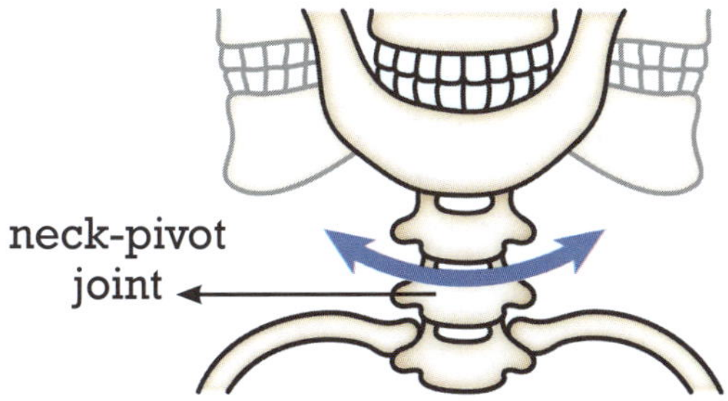

Pivot joints are found where the rounded surface of one bone fits into the ring of another. The vertebrae that allow us to nod and shake our head are examples of pivot joints.

 ISBN 978-81-8477-929-5

Quiz Time

1. Write a short note.

a. Muscle

b. Tendon

c. Ligament

d. Cartilage

2. Answer the questions.

a. Discuss the composition of bones with the help of a suitable illustration.

b. How many types of bones are there in the human body?

c. What is a joint? Name the different kinds of joints in the human body.

d. Write a short note on the spinal column.

3. Indicate whether the following statements are true (T) or false (F).

a. The shoulders and hips have ball-and-socket joints. ☐

b. At the top of the skull is the coccyx. ☐

c. The lower jawbone is the only bone in the skull that cannot move. ☐

d. Bones are joined to other bones by tendons. ☐

 ISBN 978-81-8477-929-5

4. Fill in the blanks to complete the sentences.

a. The skeletal system provides the body with ____________ and ____________.

b. ____________ and ____________ are minerals which are stored in the bones.

c. Blood cells are produced by the bone ____________ located in certain bones.

d. Bones protect the ____________ and also allow ____________.

e. Bones are made up of ____________.

f. The skull is made up of eight ____________ and ____________ facial bones.

g. There is a layer of ____________ in between each vertebra.

h. Hinged joints allow movement in one ____________.

i. Muscles help movement by ____________ and then relaxing.

j. The first seven pairs of ribs are attached in the front to the ____________.

Are human beings still evolving as a species?

 ISBN 978-81-8477-929-5

3
THE NERVOUS SYSTEM

The nervous system is the control centre of the human body. It comprises of three important parts—the brain, spinal cord and nerves.

The nervous system enables us to carry out activities such as breathing, blinking, memorising and so on.

The nervous system is divided into two main systems.

- The central nervous system
- The peripheral nervous system

THE CENTRAL NERVOUS SYSTEM

The brain and the spinal cord form the central nervous system. The brain gets information from the body and sends out instructions through nerves.

BRAIN

The brain communicates with the rest of the body through the spinal cord and the nerves. The brain is made of three main parts—the cerebrum, the cerebellum and the medulla oblongata (or the brainstem).

Factastic

The animal with the smallest brain in proportion to its body may have been the dinosaur, stegosaurus. This dinosaur weighed 1.5 tons, but its brain was only the size of a walnut.

 ISBN 978-81-8477-929-5

Cerebrum

The cerebrum or **cortex** is the largest part of the human brain. Its main functions include planning, thinking, reasoning, problem solving, movement, feeling emotions, carrying out actions, remembering and speaking.

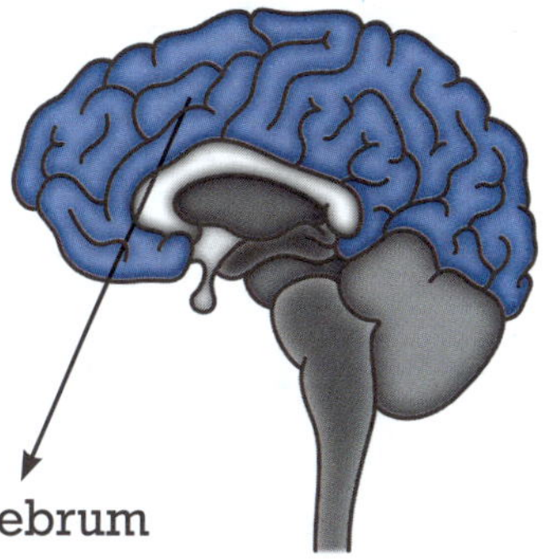

> **Factastic**
> The cerebrum makes up 85% of the brain's weight. It is the thinking part of the brain and controls the voluntary muscles. The cerebrum works to control the muscles that help us dance or walk.

The cerebrum has two halves. Scientists believe that the right half helps us think about abstract things, such as music, colours and shapes, while the left half helps us with maths, logic and speech. It is well known that the right half of the cerebrum controls the left side of the body and the left half controls the right side.

Cerebellum

The cerebellum performs functions such as regulation and coordination of movement, posture and balance. It tells us how to work all the muscles together. It is located at the back of the brain. It is also called the 'little brain' because it is only one-eighth the size of the cerebrum.

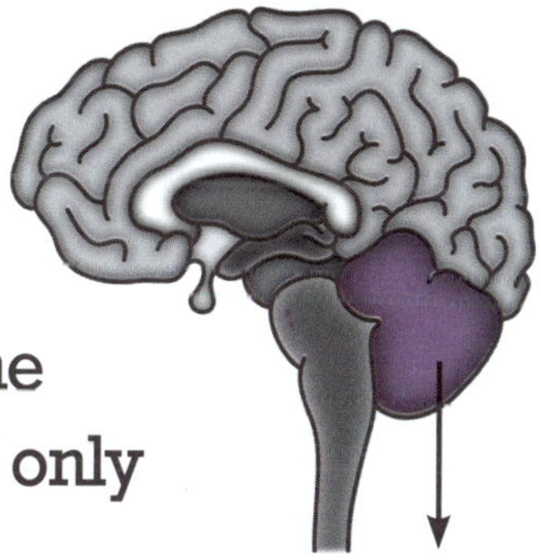

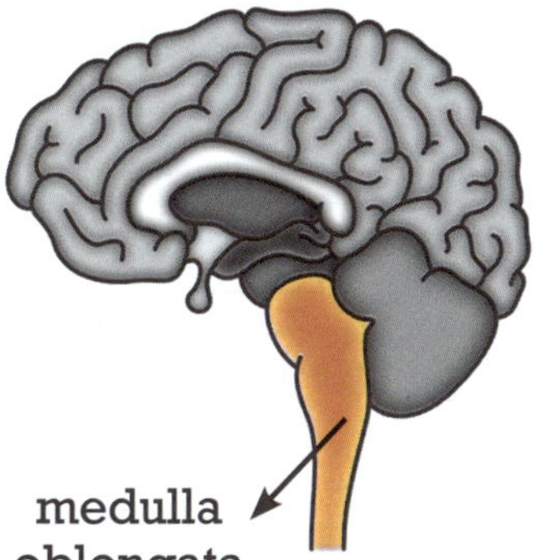

Medulla oblongata or brain stem

The medulla oblongata is responsible for vital life functions such as breathing, digesting food and blood circulation. It connects the rest of the brain to the spinal cord. It controls the involuntary muscles—the ones that work

 ISBN 978-81-8477-929-5

automatically such as the heart and the stomach.

There are two other very important parts of the brain—the pituitary gland and the hypothalamus.

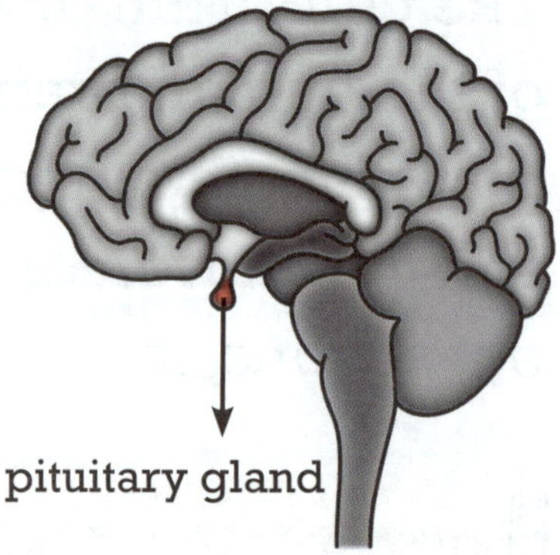

Pituitary gland

Even though the pituitary gland is very small (it is the size of a pea), it has a very important role to play. It produces and releases a hormone that controls our growth. It also controls other important hormones.

Hypothalalamus

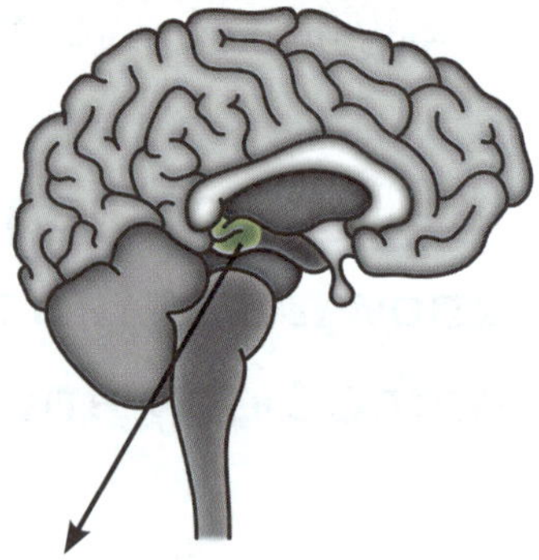

The hypothalamus controls the temperature of the body. When our environment is hot, we sweat. As the sweat evaporates, our body cools down. Similarly, if the body is too cold, the hypothalamus instructs the body to shiver and, thus, warms it up.

Explore

Objective: To understand our mind/brain and how it functions.

Materials required: Pencil, paper, an empty bowl

The words in the box list brain functions. Write them on small pieces of paper.

balancing sniffing tasting touching hearing
crying laughing smelling solving problems
drinking breathing thinking
decision making speaking

 ISBN 978-81-8477-929-5

Method: Fold the chits of paper and place them in the bowl. Divide the class into two teams—A and B. Each team will take turns to pick out a chit from the bowl and then act out the word. The team members guess and write the word on the board. Repeat the game until all the words have been identified correctly.

Spinal Cord

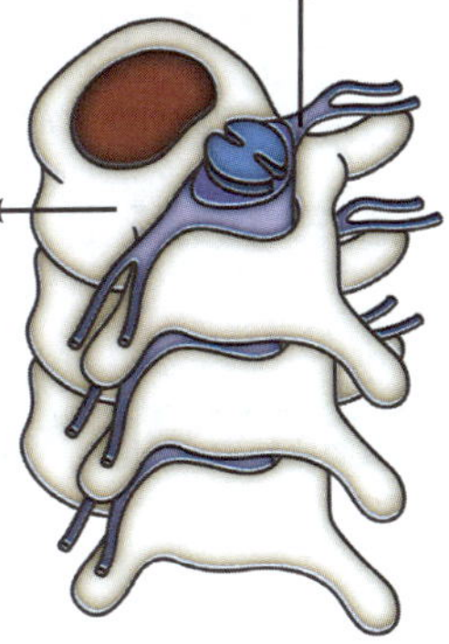

The spinal cord is a thick bundle of nerves connecting the brain to the rest of the body. It is protected by the spinal column (backbone) which protects the spinal cord from damage.

The Peripheral Nervous System

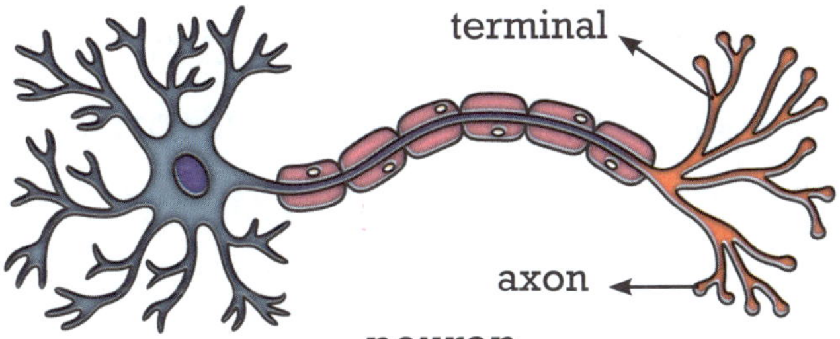

neuron

The peripheral nervous system is made up of 12 pairs of **cranial nerves** and 31 pairs of **spinal nerves**.

The cranial nerves can be seen on the ventral (bottom) surface of the brain. Some of these nerves bring information from the sense organs to the brain. Others control, or are connected to, the internal organs such as the heart and lungs.

Nerves spread through the spinal cord to the face, ears, eyes, nose and the rest of the body. They form a web within the body. Nerves divide many times as they leave the spinal cord so that they may reach all parts of the body. Nerves work as a network, gathering information from the environment, sending it to the spinal cord and then to the brain and from the brain back to the

 ISBN 978-81-8477-929-5

rest of the body. The thickest nerve is 1 inch thick and the thinnest is thinner than a human hair. Each nerve is a bundle of hundreds or thousands of **neurons** (nerve cells).

Explore

Why are we unable to walk straight and tend to lose our balance when we walk with our eyes closed? Discuss with the rest of the class.

SENSE ORGANS

The human body has five main senses—**touch**, **smell**, **taste**, **hearing** and **sight**. The skin, nose, mouth, ears and eyes are called the sense organs that help us understand and respond to the world outside the body. The sense organs send signals to the brain. The brain interprets the signals. It may send messages back to the body to respond to the signals.

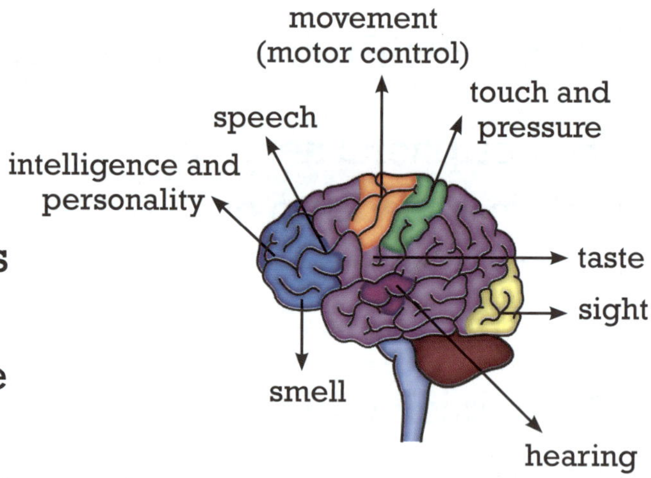

Factastic

Lizards are always flicking their tongues in and out. They taste the air and pass all the flavours back to a sense organ in their mouth.

 ISBN 978-81-8477-929-5

Quiz Time

1. Answer the questions.

a. Name the control system of the human body.

b. What is the function of the spinal cord and the nerves?

c. What is the function of the cerebrum?

d. What is the function of the cerebellum?

e. What is the function of the medulla oblongata?

f. Draw an illustration of a neuron.

g. What is the peripheral nervous system?

h. Name the five sense organs.

2. Fill in the blanks with the correct words from the brackets.

a. ________________ carries information to the brain. (Spinal cord/Heart/Lungs)

b. ________________ controls the functions of the body. (Brain/Nerves/Mouth)

c. ________________ send messages to the brain. (Nerves/Heart/Large intestine)

d The ________________ controls posture, balance, movement and coordination of muscles. (cerebrum/spine/cerebellum)

e. The ________________ controls involuntary muscles. (medulla oblongata/nerves/spinal cord)

 ISBN 978-81-8477-929-5

f. The nervous system is divided into ________________ main systems. (four/two/three)

g. Each neuron has tiny ________________ that help connect with other neurons. (branches/muscles/bones)

3. Make a drawing of your face and clearly mark the sense organs. Write the function of each organ.

4. Indicate whether the following statements are true (T) or false (F).

a. Neurons carry messages in the form of electrical impulses. ☐

b. The sense organs send signals to the brain. ☐

c. The cerebellum lies at the back of the brain, below the cerebrum. ☐

d. The cerebrum controls involuntary muscles. ☐

What is grey matter?

 ISBN 978-81-8477-929-5

4

HEALTH AND DISEASES

STAYING HEALTHY

The human body works like a complex machine that needs energy to function. Our body needs approximately fifty different nutrients and micronutrients in order to remain healthy and strong. Nutrients are found in the foods that we eat. Besides providing the body with energy, food helps the body cells to function properly. Food also helps the body fight infections and diseases.

The foods that are consumed regularly make up the diet. Different foods have different nutrients that the body requires on a regular basis. Too much or too little of some foods in the diet can be unhealthy. The body may struggle to digest or use some foods. When the body cannot use up all the food for energy, it converts food into body fat for storage. This may lead to weight gain.

There are seven categories that broadly cover our daily dietary requirements.

- Carbohydrates
- Proteins
- Fats
- Minerals
- Vitamins
- Fibre
- Water

 ISBN 978-81-8477-929-5

A Balanced Meal

A balanced meal means eating the right amount of the right type of food.

The **food pyramid** reflects the proportion in which different kinds of foods should be eaten.

Bread, other cereals and potatoes form the largest group, and are sometimes called starchy carbohydrates. This group also includes yam, pasta, rice, oats and noodles. These foods are the main energy sources for the body.

Fresh and dried fruit and vegetables form the second-largest group. These foods are important to provide the vitamins and minerals that the body needs to stay healthy. They are also an important source of fibre. We should eat five portions of fruits and vegetables a day.

Dairy foods include milk, cheese, cream and yoghurt. These foods are important for healthy bones and teeth.

Proteins include meat, poultry, fish and eggs. Alternatives include nuts, tofu, beans, such as kidney beans and canned baked beans, and pulses, such as lentils. These are important for growth and repair in the body. They are often called **muscle food** as they help build muscles.

 ISBN 978-81-8477-929-5

Fat and sugar form the smallest group indicating that they should be eaten in small quantities. The body requires only a small amount of this food group. Fat provides energy and heat to the body. The body also needs fat for many cell functions and for brain activity. Sources of fat include butter, cheese, milk, cream, oil, nuts and seeds.

Keeping the Body Healthy

Water

The body needs plenty of water to keep it functioning well. Water makes up about 60% of the body weight. Every cell in the body depends on water to work properly. Water forms a major part of the body fluids such as blood, digestive juices, sweat and urine.

When the body does not get enough water, it gets dehydrated. Dehydration slows down the body's processes. It interrupts the working of the body's cells and organs.

Besides drinking water, the body gets water from fluids such as milk, soup and juice. Foods such a fruits and vegetables also contain a lot of water.

Exercise

Along with a balanced diet, the body requires regular exercise. Regular exercise helps develop muscles. It increases the heart rate and improves the circulation of blood in the body. Exercise also improves the flexibility of the joints. It helps build immunity and protects the body from diseases.

 ISBN 978-81-8477-929-5

Many diseases are linked to improper diets and lack of exercise. They include heart attacks or strokes, high or low blood pressure, high cholesterol and diabetes.

Rest

Regular hours of sleep and rest are important for the body. During sleep, the body shuts down many of its systems. The muscles relax. The body's cells are able to function properly.

DISEASES

A disease is an interruption in the normal functioning of the body due to a specific cause. Diseases have identifiable symptoms.

There are different types of diseases, but they can be broadly categorised into communicable and non-communicable diseases.

 ISBN 978-81-8477-929-5

Explore

Discuss with the class how the H1N1 virus (or the swine flu) is spreading across the world. What are its causes? How is it passed on from one infected person to another? Find out the difference between an epidemic and a pandemic.

Communicable Diseases

Communicable diseases are caused by germs or micro-organisms. The infection can be transmitted from one infected person to another. These infections can also be transmitted from infected animals to humans.

- The germs of diseases such as scarlet fever, measles, mumps, whooping cough, influenza and diphtheria **spread through air**. They can be expelled from the nose or mouth of the infected person and be inhaled by another.
- Some communicable diseases, such as cholera, typhoid and dysentery, **spread through contaminated food** or **water**.
- Some infections, such as malaria, dengue, plague and rabies, are transmitted to humans by **animals or insects**.
- An injury in the presence of infected soil or dirt may cause tetanus.
- Use of infected medical instruments or transfusion of infected blood may cause hepatitis.
- Tuberculosis may be transmitted by an infected individual to a healthy one by air and by sharing food or utensils.
- AIDS (Acquired Immune Deficiency Syndrome) is a communicable disease of the immune system caused by a virus. A healthy individual can contract the disease if AIDS-infected blood or body fluids enter his or her body.

 ISBN 978-81-8477-929-5

communicable disease and how it spreads	symptoms
Cholera usually spreads by eating food or drinking water that is contaminated	• Diarrhoea • Vomiting • Cramps in the legs • Thirst
Typhoid is transmitted by the ingestion of food or water contaminated with the faeces	• Severe headache • Fever with low pulse • Dry, white, coated tongue
Influenza (flu) spreads through air in tiny droplets caused by coughing and sneezing	• Fever • Cold, cough and sneezing • Headache, bodyache and nausea
Tuberculosis spreads through the air when an infected person coughs or sneezes	• Persistent cough • Loss of appetite and weight • Excessive weakness • Rapid pulse and chest pain
Malaria spreads when a person is bitten by a female mosquito, the parasite enters the bloodstream via the mosquito's saliva	• Fever • Alternating chill and perspiration • Headache and bodyache • Nausea and vomiting
Tetanus spreads through a puncture or wound that is exposed to soil/dust or a rusted object	• Restlessness, headache and fever • Stiff neck • Difficulty in chewing and swallowing • Muscle spasms in the jaw and face • Bending of back in the shape of a bow • Severe pain

ISBN 978-81-8477-929-5

The prevention and control of communicable diseases is possible. It requires education and increased awareness in matters of personal as well as community responsibility. Some of these diseases can also be prevented by vaccination.

> **Factastic**
> Malaria is caused by a parasite known as *plasmodium*, which is transmitted by the bite of the *anopheles* mosquito. The parasite multiplies in the liver of the human body and then attacks the red blood cells.

Learn More

Ask your parents for your vaccination card. Bring it to class and discuss the vaccinations you have received and for which diseases.

Non-Communicable Diseases

Non-communicable diseases are not infectious because they cannot be passed on from one person to another. They are caused due to unhealthy diets, factors involving the environment or genetic factors. Non-communicable diseases are also known as chronic diseases. These diseases generally last a long duration but may progress slowly. Examples of non-communicable diseases include heart disease, diabetes, asthma and cancer.

Heart disease is linked to a diet that is high in unhealthy fats. There are different kinds of fats. Animal products, such as meat, eggs and cheese are high in fats called saturated fats. Unsaturated fats raise the level of cholesterol in the body. Cholesterol is a fatty substance that is found in the blood vessels. Too much cholesterol in the blood clogs up the blood vessels. Clogged blood vessels may reduce or even stop blood flow, causing heart disease.

 ISBN 978-81-8477-929-5

Diabetes is a disease related to the hormone, insulin, in the body. Insulin helps the body store and use sugar and fat from food. People with diabetes either don't make insulin or their body cells are resistant to insulin. It leads to high levels of sugar in the blood.

Factastic

Diabetes is a major cause of blindness, kidney failure and limb amputations leading to admissions in hospitals. Diabetes and hypertension contribute to heart disease and stroke.

Asthma is a disease that affects the bronchial tubes in the body. These tubes lead from the windpipe into the lungs. People with asthma get an asthma attack or episode during which their bronchial tubes get swollen and narrower. This blocks the passage of air in and out of the lungs.

Cancer is a term used for diseases in which cells that are not normal grow and spread very fast in the body. These abnormal cells divide without control and are able to invade other tissues. They group or clump together to form tumours. A tumour becomes a lump of cancer cells that can destroy the normal cells in the body and damage the body's healthy tissues. Sometimes cancer cells travel to other areas of the body and form new tumours.

 ISBN 978-81-8477-929-5

name of the disease	due to the deficiency of	symptoms	can be prevented by the intake of
Night blindness	Vitamin A	Inability to see in the dark	Green leafy vegetables, tomato, papaya, mango, butter, milk, fish and egg yolk
Beriberi	Vitamin B	Lethargy and fatigue	Unpolished rice
Scurvy 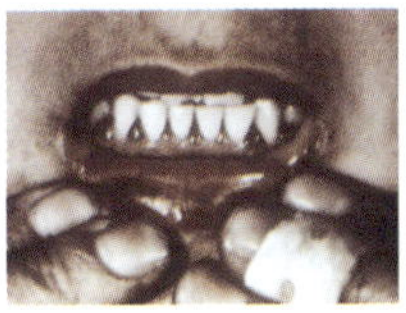	Vitamin C	Bleeding of gums and swelling of joints	Citrus fruits such as oranges and lime, strawberries, amla, tomatoes, broccoli, potatoes and sprouted grains
Rickets 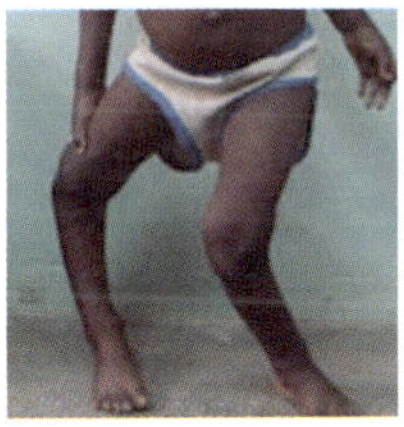	Vitamin D	Softening of the bones	Oily fish, liver, cod liver oil, dairy products, sunlight, calcium and phosphorus
Goitre 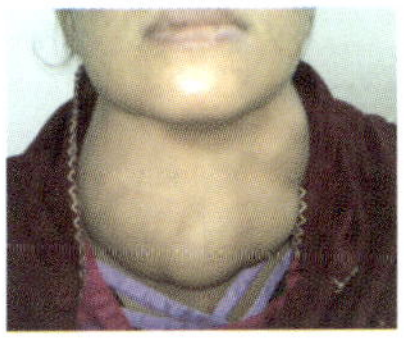	Iodine	Swelling of the front part of the neck and protruding eyes	Iodised salt and sea food
Anaemia 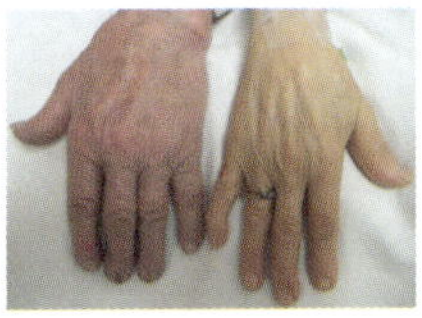	Iron	Reduced haemoglobin, which reduces the amount of oxygen in the blood	Pulses, spinach, apples, bananas, guavas, jaggery, liver and meat

 ISBN 978-81-8477-929-5

Chronic diseases are largely preventable by effective interventions that deal with the risk factors such as use of tobacco and alcohol, unhealthy diet and low physical activity.

Vaccination

Some diseases can be prevented with the help of vaccinations. A **vaccine** is a small amount of weakened disease-causing germs. It is swallowed or injected into the body. The body cells respond to the weakened germs by producing antibodies. **Antibodies** help fight the infection. Antibodies remain in the blood and guard the body against any future attacks by the same germs. The body develops immunity against the disease the germs cause.

Vaccines are available for several diseases including cholera, diphtheria, influenza, measles, mumps, small pox, pertussis, tetanus and typhoid.

Quiz Time

1. Answer the questions.

a. What is a balanced meal?

b. Why is it essential to exercise and take proper rest?

c. What are the effects of a poor or unhealthy diet?

d. What is the difference between communicable and non-communicable diseases?

e. What is a deficiency disease?

 ISBN 978-81-8477-929-5

2. Answer in one sentence.

a. What causes anaemia?

b. What disease is caused due to the lack of iodine?

c. What is rickets?

d. What is an infectious disease?

3. Indicate whether the following statements are true (T) or false (F).

a. Proteins are important for growth and repair of body tissues. ☐

b. Carbohydrates help the body store and use sugar and fat from food. ☐

c. Cancer cells grow and divide out of control. ☐

d. Typhoid is a non-communicable disease. ☐

4. Fill in the blanks with the correct words from the brackets.

a. ________________ fats raise the level of cholesterol in the body. (Unsaturated/Dissaturated/Saturated)

b. Dehydration ________________ the body's processes. (slows down/shuts down/speeds up)

c. Sugar is a kind of ________________. (vitamin/carbohydrate/starch)

d. Influenza and tuberculosis are ________________ diseases. (miscommunicable/communicable/non-communicable)

Why do doctors prescribe some medicines to be taken before and some after food?

 ISBN 978-81-8477-929-5

5

How Do Plants Reproduce?

Plants can be divided into two types.

- **Flowering plants** such as rose, sunflowers and marigold.
- **Non-flowering plants** such as the pine and spruce.

Plants that bear flowers are called flowering plants. Flowers play an important role in making seeds.

A typical flower is made up of four different parts.

Calyx is the outermost part of a flower. It is usually green in colour. The individual parts of the calyx are called **sepals**. The sepals help protect a young flower at the bud stage.

Corolla consists of petals that are brightly coloured to attract animals for pollination.

Androecium is the male part and is made up of **stamens** that have a **filament** with an **anther** on top. Pollens are produced in the anther.

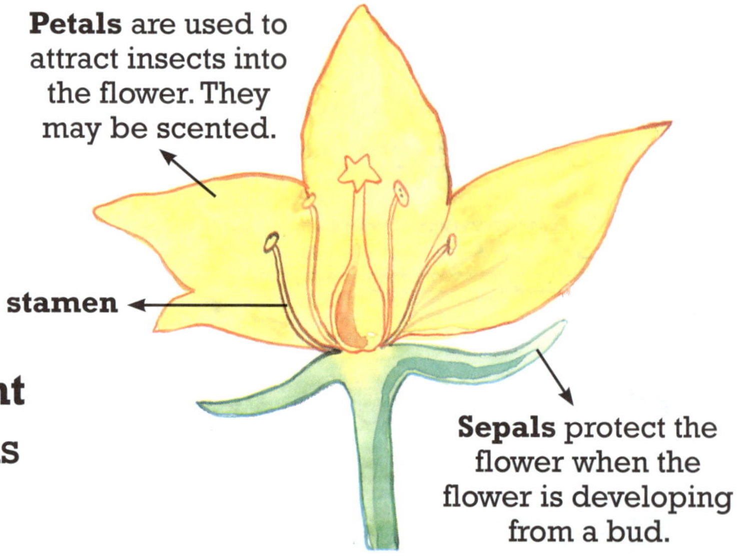

 ISBN 978-81-8477-929-5

Gynoecium is the female part and is made up of carpels. Each carpel includes an ovary containing ovules, a style and a stigma. Pistal is the collective term of the carpel(s). After fertilisation, the ovary grows into a fruit and each ovule grows into a seed.

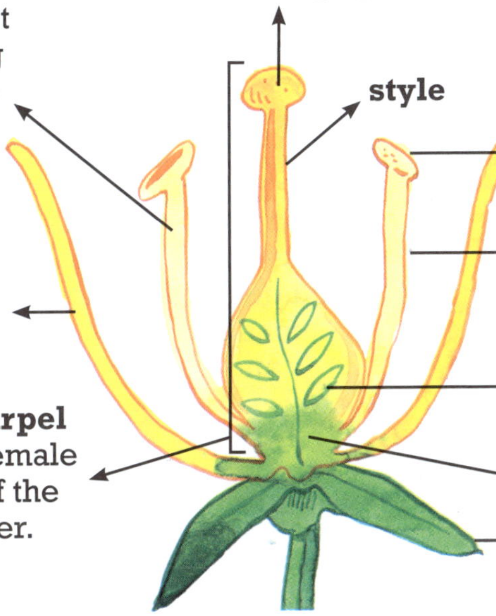

cross-section of a flower

POLLINATION

Pollen from a plant is carried by the wind, or by insects, to fertilise the female parts of the plant. Once fertilised, a seed is produced which in turn can create a new plant. This process is known as **pollination**.

When pollination occurs, pollen moves from a stamen to the stigma. The plants must be of the same species. For example, only pollen from a sunflower can pollinate another sunflower.

 ISBN 978-81-8477-929-5

Types of Pollination

When pollen from a plant's stamen is transferred to the stigma of the same plant, it is known as **self-pollination**. When pollen from a plant's stamen is transferred to the stigma of a different plant, it is known as **cross-pollination**. Grains of pollen land on the stigma. Then a tiny tube grows from it and down the style into the ovary. Nuclei from the pollen grain fuse with nuclei in the ovule. This is called **fertilisation**. The fertilised ovule becomes the seed and the ovary becomes the fruit.

Means of Pollination

Plants rely on birds, insects, animals or the wind to pollinate them.

Birds and **insects**, such as bees, butterflies and flies, are attracted to the sweet nectar at the base of the petals. When they come to feed on a plant, the sticky pollen gets attached to their bodies as they rub against the stamen. As they move to another flower to feed, some of the pollen falls off their body on to the stigma of the new plant.

When collecting nectar an insect brushes against stamens and pollen sticks to its legs and body.

When the insect visits another flower, pollen brushes from its body against the stigma.

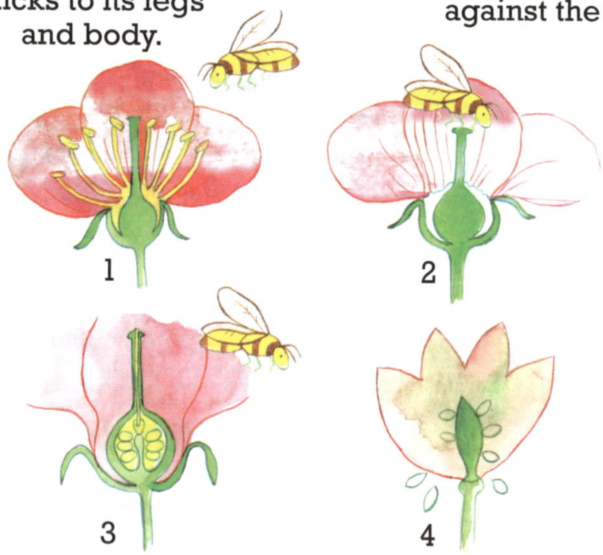

The pollen passes down the stigma to the ovum where it fertilises the seeds.

When the seeds are ripe they disperse. If they land on moist, light ground, a new plant will grow.

Animals are often attracted to the strong scent and the bright colours of flowers. These animal pollinators also help plants as they go from plant to plant in search of food.

 ISBN 978-81-8477-929-5

Sometimes, **wind** picks up the pollen from one plant and transfers it to another resulting in **wind pollination**. Plants pollinated by wind often have long stamens and pistils. They may not be brightly coloured. They have small petals or none at all.

NEW PLANTS FROM SEEDS

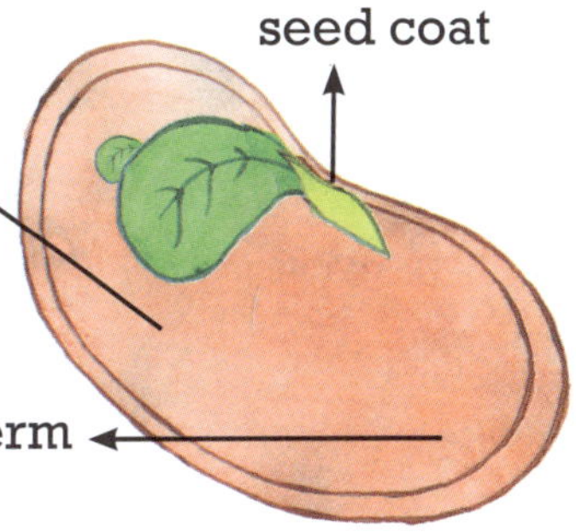

The fertilised ovule forms the seed. The outer covering of a seed is called the **seed coat**. Seed coats help protect the **embryo**. Seed coats can be thin and soft like the seed coat in beans. They can be thick and hard like the seed coat in coconuts.

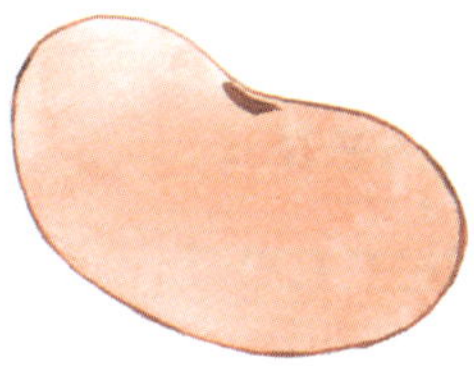

The seed coat protects the embryo within it and also prevents the seed from dying.

The **endosperm** is the food stored within the seed, which is used by the embryo for its development. This temporary supply of food is in the form of special leaves, known as **seed leaves** or **cotyledons**. These are generally the first parts visible when the seed germinates.

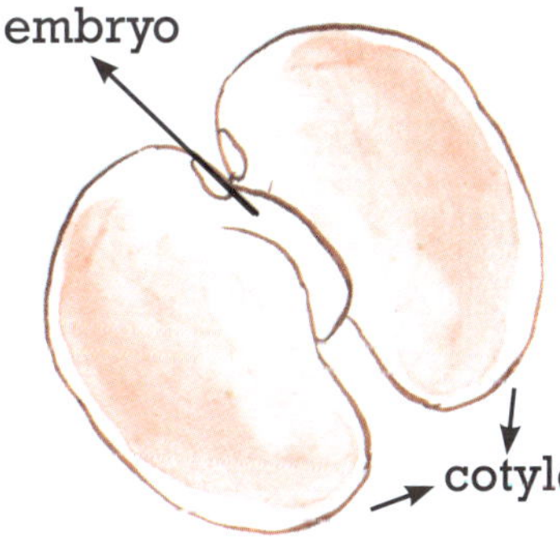

Plants are classified depending on the number of cotyledons or seed leaves they have. A plant with only one cotyledon is known as a **monocotyledon** (**monocot**). Grass and corn are monocots. A plant with two cotyledons is known as a **dicotyledon** (**dicot**). Beans are dicots.

monocot and dicot

 ISBN 978-81-8477-929-5

The process of growth of the embryo plant inside the seed is known as **germination**.

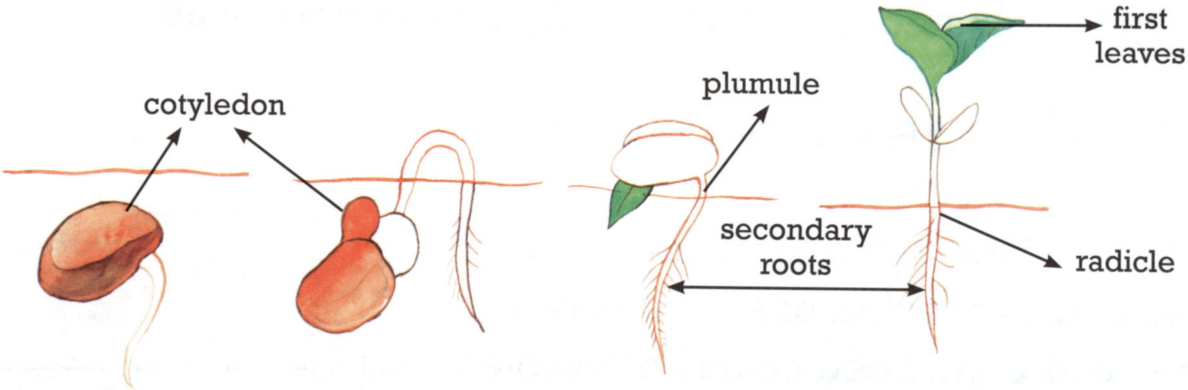

Seeds remain dormant or inactive until conditions are right for germination. All seeds need a certain amount of water, oxygen, sunlight and temperature to germinate. Water and oxygen are taken in through the seed coat.

As the embryo starts to develop, the seed coat breaks open and a root or **radicle** emerges. The seed coat swells and breaks open. First, a root or radicle emerges and then, the shoot or plumule emerges. The shoot contains the leaves and stem of the new plant.

The seedling's stem and the cotyledons grow upwards and the roots extend downwards.

Seed Dispersal

It is very important that seeds are dispersed over a wide area. If all the seeds fell and grew beneath the parent plant, it would cause overcrowding. The seeds would have to struggle for space, air, water, nutrients and sunlight. Hence, seed dispersal ensures that all seeds get a better chance of finding the right conditions to grow in.

 ISBN 978-81-8477-929-5

Seeds are dispersed in various ways to form new plants.

Wind dispersal

Some seeds that are very light in weight are carried away from the parent plant with the help of wind. These include orchid and poppy seeds. Some seeds, such as dandelions, have hair-like growths that catch the wind and help carry the seeds away from the parent plant.

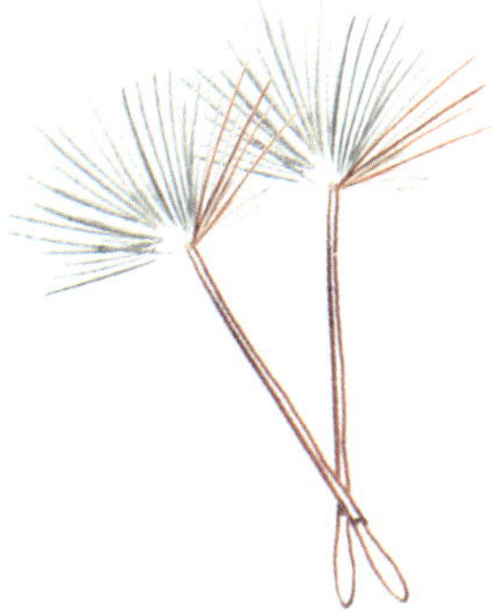

dandelion

> **Factastic**
> Coconuts may get carried away for thousands of kilometres across the seas and oceans.

Water dispersal

Some seeds are hollow and they get carried away by water. These include coconut and palm seeds.

Animal dispersal

Fruits form a part of the diet of some animals. While only the pulp of the fruit is digested, the seeds (or the pips and stones) get passed out of their digestive system and are, thus, dispersed.

> **Factastic**
> To prepare for the cold winter months, squirrels collect acorns and bury them. The squirrels often forget about these acorns, which then grow into oak trees.

The seeds of sea holly and the burdock plant have hooks on them, which get attached to the fur of animals. The animals later shake off these seeds far from the parent plant and, thus, help in seed dispersal.

burdock

sea holly

Dispersal by explosion

Some plants, such as broom, peas and beans, have pods that explode as they ripen. This explosion helps to scatter the seeds.

broom

 ISBN 978-81-8477-929-5

Dispersal by gravity

Large, heavy fruits, such as coconuts, just drop off the tree on to the ground as they ripen. These fruits can then be carried away from the parent plant by animals, by water or they might just simply roll away. Very often, their soft skin may burst open to scatter the seeds inside.

Vegetative Reproduction

Many plants can grow from plant parts such as stems, roots and leaves. The process of growing new plants from existing plant parts is called vegetative reproduction.

New plants emerge from the roots of the dandelion plant.

Garlic is a special type of a stem. It can be used to grow a new plant.

Tubers have buds that grow into roots and shoots to produce a new plant. Potatoes are an example of tubers.

Runners are stems that run along the ground and **rhizomes** are stems that spread underground. New plants grow from the tips of runners. Strawberry is an example. Many grasses and weeds are spread by rhizomes.

Some fruit trees and bushes send up new shoots from the roots. These are called **suckers**. Apples and raspberries are examples of suckers.

bryophyllum

In some plants, such as bryophyllum (air plant), tiny plantlets grow along leaf

 ISBN 978-81-8477-929-5

margins. When the leaves fall off, the new plants grow independently.

Some plants don't produce flowers and seeds. They produce spores instead of seeds. Ferns and mosses are examples. The parent plant produces spores that are stored in spore cases until they are ripe. Then the parent plant releases the spores. The spores grow into a tiny prothallus, which produces sperm cells and eggs. When water is available, the sperm swims to an egg and fertilizes it. The embryo grows into a new plant.

spores on ferns

A **graft** is used to reproduce varieties that are difficult to grow, such as apples, pears, hibiscus and rose. Grafting literally means joining parts of two or more plants together such that they grow as one plant.

grafting

prothallus: a small, greenish heart-shaped structure of a fern

ISBN 978-81-8477-929-5

Learn More

Use an encyclopedia to find out what a bonsai is.

PLANT ADAPTATIONS

Like animals, plants also adapt in order to survive in different climatic conditions.

A desert is usually hot and dry. The soil is often sandy or rocky and unable to retain water. In order to cope with the scarcity of water, some plants store water in their stems or leaves. Plants, such as cacti, have bulbous stems that store water.

cacti

Desert plants have spines rather than leaves. They have light-coloured hair that helps shade them and hence reduce water loss.

In regions of excessive rainfall, there is a risk of flooding, soil erosion and loss of nutrients from the soil. Plants in such regions have flowers and leaves coated with a wax-like substance, which does not allow water to stay on it. The water slides off easily. Plants in these regions have shallow roots, which absorb nutrients from the top of the soil.

The roots of plants, such as mangroves, that are found in wet marshlands, are propped up, as if on stilts, so that water does not collect under them.

mangroves

 ISBN 978-81-8477-929-5

Aquatic plants have underwater leaves and stems that are flexible and can move with water currents. Some aquatic plants have air spaces in their stems to help hold the plant up in the water. The plants absorb nutrients through their leaves directly from the water. Some plants have leaves that float on the water to catch sunlight. Floating plants have chlorophyll only on the upper surface of leaves which receive sunlight. The upper surface has a waxy coating that keeps water off. Many aquatic plants produce seeds that can float.

aquatic plants

Circle Time

Divide the class into groups of five. Create charts on how plants contribute to the environment.

Quiz Time

1. Write a short note.

a. Stigma

b. Style

c. Pistil

d. Anther

e. Stamen

 ISBN 978-81-8477-929-5

2. Answer the questions.

a. What is pollination? Explain with the help of illustrations.

b. What are the different ways in which pollination takes place?

c. What is a seed?

d. What is germination?

e. What is seed dispersal? What are the different methods in which seeds are dispersed?

f. How do plants adapt to the following habitats?

   i. dry deserts
   ii. regions with heavy rainfall
   iii. wet marshlands

3. Fill in the blanks with the correct words from the brackets.

a. Pollen from a plant is carried by wind or insects to fertilise the female parts of the plant to form a ______________. (roots/seed/flower)

b. The male part of a flower is made up of ______________. (stamens/seeds/flowers)

c. Plants pollinated by wind have ______________ stamens. (thick/short/long)

d. Garlic is a special type of ______________. (stem/root/leaf)

e. A ______________ is used to reproduce different varieties of roses. (bryophyllum/spores/graft)

f. Roots of mangroves are propped up so that ______________ does not collect under them. (sand/water/stone)

 ISBN 978-81-8477-929-5

4. Indicate whether the following statements are true (T) or false (F).

a. Deciduous trees shed their leaves in the autumn and grow new ones in spring. ☐

b. The androecium is the food packed around the embryo. ☐

c. Tubers have buds that grow into roots and shoots to produce a new plant. ☐

d. Seeds are made in the cotyledons. ☐

Is there a way to prolong the life of fresh cut flowers?

 ISBN 978-81-8477-929-5

6
MATTER

Everything around us is made up of molecules that occupy space. Everything that has mass and occupies space is known as **matter**.

Mass is a measure of how much there is of an object. Air, water, rocks, plants and metals are all examples of matter.

A **phase** describes the physical state of matter. The phase or state of matter can change when the temperature changes. Generally, as the temperature rises, matter assumes a more active state since energy is added. Matter changes states through freezing, melting, evaporation and condensation.

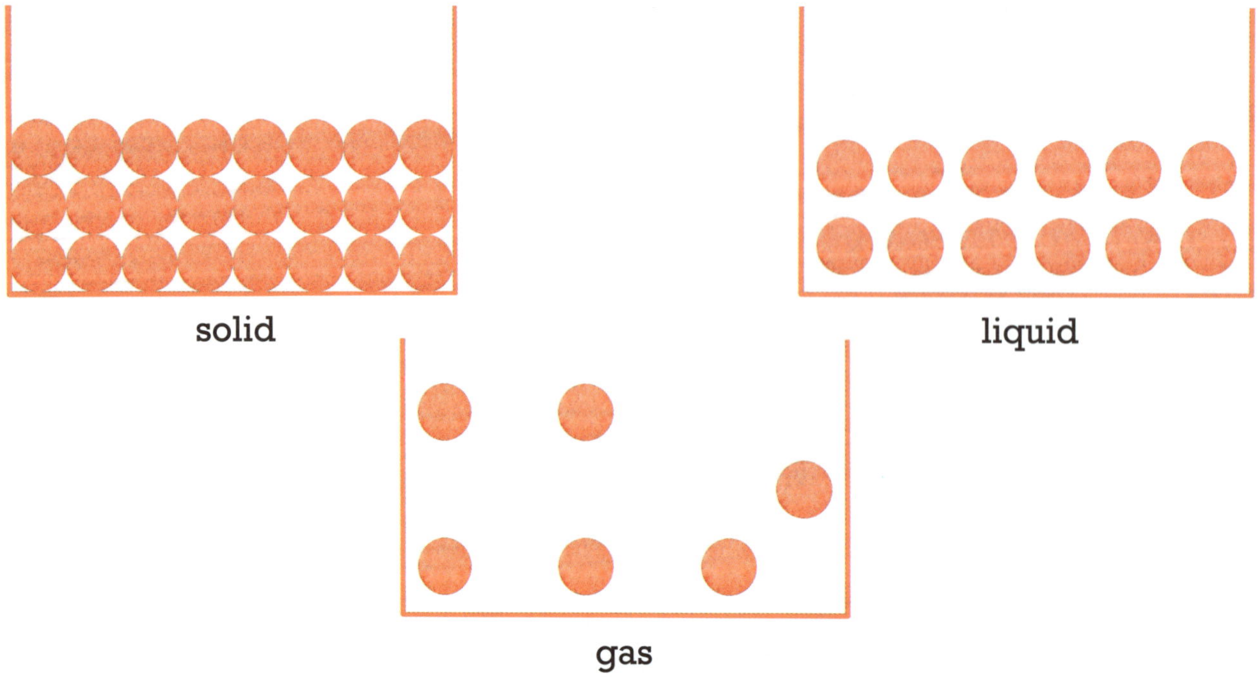

 ISBN 978-81-8477-929-5

CHARACTERISTICS OF GASES, LIQUIDS AND SOLIDS

solid	liquid	gas
Retains a fixed volume and shape independent of the container	Takes the shape of the part of the container that it occupies	Takes the shape and volume of its container
There is very little free space between molecules. It is very difficult to compress	Not too much free space between the molecules. It cannot be compressed easily	Plenty of free space between the molecules. It can be compressed
It is very rigid. Its molecules cannot move or slide past one another, that is, it does not flow easily	Its molecules can move or slide past one another	Its molecules can move past one another, that is, it flows easily
Its molecules are tightly packed usually in a regular pattern	Its molecules are close together with no special arrangement	Its molecules are separated with no regular arrangement

No matter what phase or physical state water is in, it will always be water. This means that when water vapour changes to water and then freezes to form ice, no chemical change takes place. It is only a physical change.

Learn More

Take equal amounts of different kinds of liquids such as water, milk, apple juice, tea and sugar syrup. Observe how long it will take for these liquids to freeze.

 ISBN 978-81-8477-929-5

Change of State

Matter can change from one physical state to another.

The change of state from solid to liquid is known as **melting**.

The change of state from liquid to solid is known as **solidification**.

The change of state from liquid to gas is known as **vapourisation**.

The change of state from gas to liquid is known as **condensation**.

Explore

Objective: To observe reversible and irreversible changes.

Method A: Mix a small quantity of each of these solids with water. Observe what happens and complete the chart.

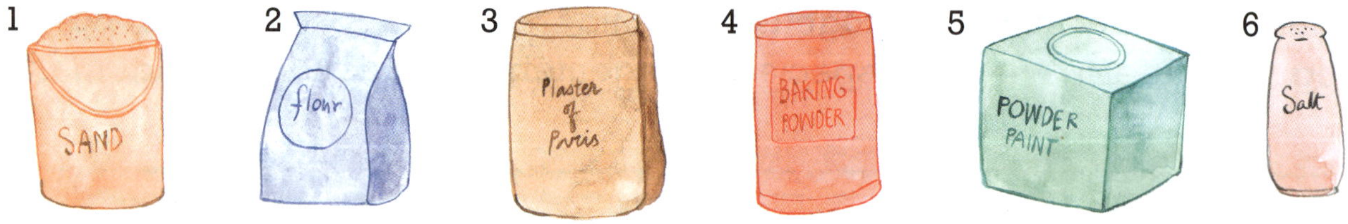

Observation: ____________________

	dissolves in water	does not dissolve in water	there appears to be a different sort of change
1			
2			
3			

 ISBN 978-81-8477-929-5

	dissolves in water	does not dissolve in water	there appears to be a different sort of change
4			
5			
6			

Method B: You might try some other mixes (use gloves)

- cement and water
- lemon juice and washing soda
- vinegar and baking soda

Observation: ____

	process	reversible change	irreversible change
ice 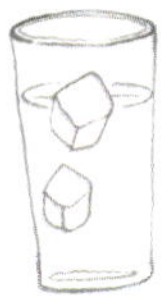	heat	✓	
paper 	burn		✓
egg 	heat		✓
bread/ dough 	heat		✓
clay 	heat		✓

 ISBN 978-81-8477-929-5

	process	reversible change	irreversible change
milk 	heat		✓
chocolate 	heat		✓
candle 	burn	✓	
cake 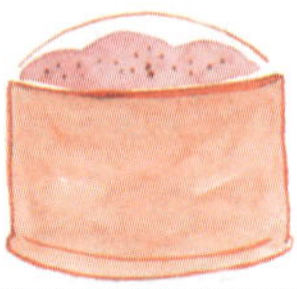	heat		✓
wood 	burn		✓

Circle Time

Find out why ice floats on water. Discuss with the rest of the class how icebergs stay afloat.

Quiz Time

1. Answer in one word.

a. Which of the three states of matter has a definite volume?

b. Which of the three states of matter has a definite shape?

c. Which of the three states of matter is easily compressed?

d. Which of the three states of matter flows easily?

 ISBN 978-81-8477-929-5

e. What kind of energy transfer is almost always involved in changes of state?

f. What is the process called when a solid becomes a liquid?

g. What is the process called when a liquid becomes a gas?

h. What is the process called when a liquid becomes a solid?

i. What is the process called when a gas becomes a liquid?

2. Answer the questions.

a. What are the different states of matter?

b. Give two examples of substances in each of the three different states of matter.

c. What is the difference between a physical and a chemical change?

d. Explain the terms solidification and vapourisation.

e. Do physical changes chemically alter the molecules involved?

f. List three differences between solids, liquids and gases.

3. Indicate whether the following statements are true (T) or false (F).

a. In a physical change, the new substance has the same properties as the original one. ☐

b. The change of state from gas to liquid is called condensation. ☐

c. Gases are the most dense of the three states of matter. ☐

d. Liquids are fluid and can flow, be poured and spilled. ☐

 ISBN 978-81-8477-929-5

4. Gases can be used in many ways. Look up an encylopedia and find out which gas is used in the following.

______________________ ______________________

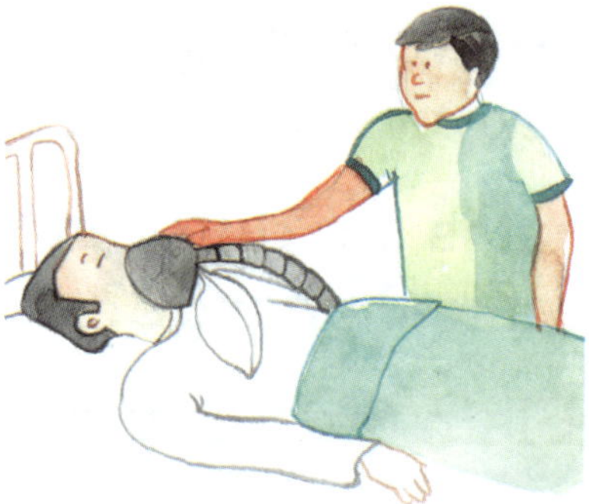

______________________ ______________________

5. Fill in the blanks with the correct words from the brackets.

a. A ______________ has a definite shape and a fixed volume. (gas/liquid/solid)

b. ______________ is how easily something burns. (Boiling/Oxidation/Flammability)

c. Chemical changes are usually ______________. (reversible/ permanent/irreversible)

d. Gases ______________ be compressed. (can/must/cannot)

How does wheat flour become malleable and elastic when mixed with water?

 ISBN 978-81-8477-929-5

7

ROCKS, MINERALS AND SOIL

Earth is a rocky planet. Scientists believe it formed from melted rock billions of years ago. It cooled over time forming a crust on the outside. The outer surface, or **crust**, of the Earth is a layer of thin rock. Beneath the crust is a thick layer of hot, molten rock. This is called the **mantle**. Beneath the mantle and at the centre of the Earth is the **core**.

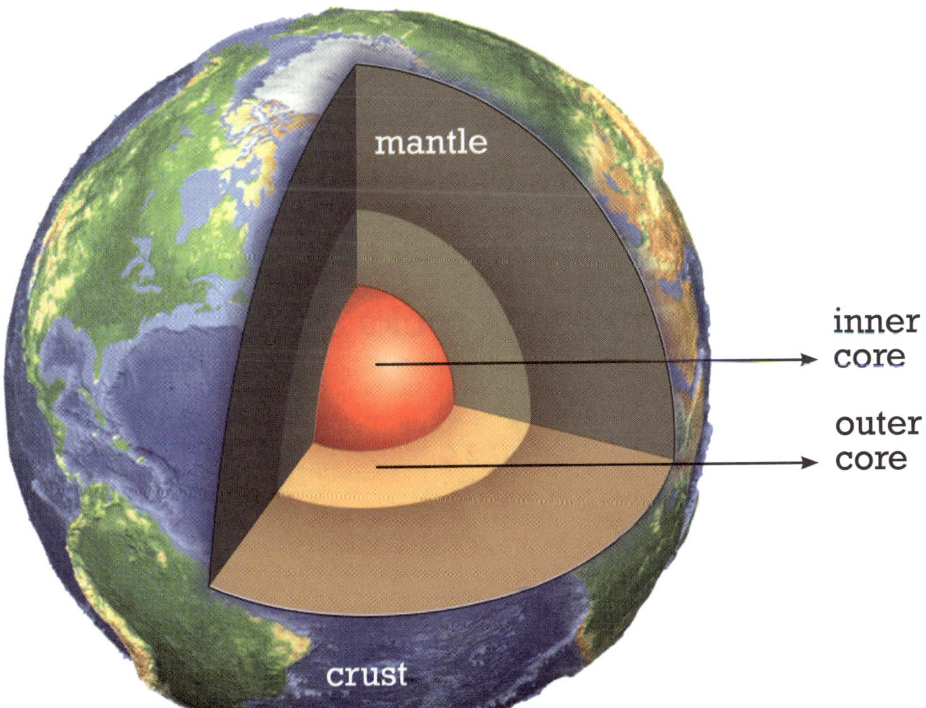

 ISBN 978-81-8477-929-5

ROCKS

The hard material of the Earth's crust exposed on the surface or present right under the soil is called rock. Rocks are a combination of two or more minerals. We use rocks in our everyday lives in various ways.

TYPES OF ROCKS

Rocks are classified depending on their method of formation.

Igneous rocks

During a volcanic eruption, the molten rock or magma flows out from deep under the Earth's crust. As the magma cools down and solidifies, it forms igneous rocks. Igneous rocks are also known as **fire rocks**. These fire rocks are formed under the ground as well as above it.

Igneous rocks formed above the surface of the Earth are known as **volcanic rocks** or **extrusive igneous rocks**. For example, pumice and scoria.

Some rocks, such as granite and pegmatite, solidify below the surface of the Earth. These rocks are known as **intrusive** or **plutonic rocks**.

 ISBN 978-81-8477-929-5

rock	characteristics	type of rock	uses
Granite 	Very hard rock	Plutonic rock; formed under the surface of the Earth in underground air chambers	Statues, monuments, slabs, shelves and floorings
Pumice 	Very light. It can float in water as it has many air pockets in it	Volcanic rock; formed as the lava cools down above the surface of the Earth	• Coarse material in hand soaps and emery boards • Landscaping gardens
Obsidian 	Glassy and smooth, with very sharp edges	Volcanic rock; formed as the lava cools quickly above the surface of the Earth	Jewellery and ornaments
Scoria 	Glassy with many air pockets visible on its surface	Volcanic rock; formed as lava cools quickly above the surface	Decorative stones

Explore

Objective: To make our own edible igneous rocks.

Materials required: 1 tin of condensed milk, 1 cup peanuts, 1 cup marshmallows, 1 cup chocolate cookies

Method: Mix all the ingredients together and refrigerate. Scoop out chunks of igneous rocks and enjoy.

 ISBN 978-81-8477-929-5

Sedimentary rocks

For millions of years, the mountains and rocks have been eroded by wind and water. These tiny pieces are washed down by water and they settle at the bottom of rivers, lakes, seas and oceans. As layer over layer of the eroded rocks is deposited on top of each other, they get compressed over time until they turn back into rocks. These rocks are known as sedimentary rocks.

Sedimentary rocks often have fossils in them. Plants and animals that have died get covered up by layers of sediment. Most of the fossils in sedimentary rocks are of plants and animals that lived in the water.

rock	characteristics	uses
Sandstone 	Made from small grains of quartz and feldspar	Building stones
Limestone 	Made from mineral calcite and sea animal shells	Building stones
Shale 	Made from compacted clay. It may contain fossils	• Building material • Manufacture of cement, lime and paper
Conglomerate 	Made from sand and pebbles (as the sediments are very large, they are cemented together with sea minerals)	Bricks

 ISBN 978-81-8477-929-5

rock	characteristics	uses
Gypsum 	Formed as a result of evaporating seawater	Plaster of Paris
Coal 	Formed from plant material (fossils)	• Fuel • In power plants to generate electricity

Learn More

Is it possible that the sand that we see on the beach today may become a sedimentary rock some day? Use an encyclopedia to research the possibilities.

Explore

Objective: To make our own edible sedimentary rocks.

Materials required: 1 tin of condensed milk, 1 cup peanuts, 1 cup cornflakes, 1 cup biscuit crumbs, 1 cup coconut flakes

Method: Sprinkle all the different ingredients layer by layer. Pour the condensed milk in the end. Freeze well. Enjoy the sedimentary rocks.

Metamorphic rocks

Metamorphic rocks are formed as a result of changes in other rocks. They form from igneous, sedimentary or other metamorphic rocks that have changed over time. Slate, marble and quartzite are examples of metamorphic rocks.

 ISBN 978-81-8477-929-5

The minerals in the original rocks change as a result of heat and pressure. When the Earth's crust moves, it causes some rocks to get compressed. This produces a lot of heat that causes the rock to change. Sedimentary rocks limestone and shale become marble and slate, respectively, when metamorphosed.

rock	characteristics	uses
Schist 	Formed from shale (a sedimentary rock)	Building material
Gneiss 	Formed from granite (an igneous rock)	Building stones
Marble 	Formed from limestone (a sedimentary rock)	Statues, structures, flooring tiles and counter tops
Slate 	Formed from shale (a sedimentary rock)	Bricks and cement
Quartzite 	Composed primarily of quartz. It is formed from sandstone (a sedimentary rock)	Jewellery and ornaments

 ISBN 978-81-8477-929-5

How Rocks Change

Weathering

All rocks on Earth break up into smaller pieces over time. This process is called weathering. Hot and cold temperatures affect weathering of rocks. Rainwater can freeze and expand in cracks in the rock. Over time, this may cause rocks to crack and break up. Sometimes, chemicals in water may dissolve rock and cause it to break up. Some types of rocks dissolve in water. Acid rain also causes weathering of rocks. Tree roots can grow into small cracks in the rocks and in time break them apart.

Erosion

As rocks weather, they get broken up into small pieces or particles. The particles are transported to different places. The movement of weathered particles is called erosion.

Erosion occurs in different ways. Broken pieces of rock can fall down mountain and hill slopes. Rivers and streams transport weathered particles as they flow. Small grains of rock are picked up and moved by wind in dust storms. Glaciers also transport large pieces of stone from one place to another.

Deposition

Particles of rock that are eroded finally land or get deposited at a place. This is called deposition. Rivers carry sediments that get deposited along their course. Similarly, winds deposit grains of rocks at different places. Melting glaciers also deposit eroded rocks.

ISBN 978-81-8477-929-5

During deposition, rock particles are deposited in layers. Heavier particles are dumped first and then covered by finer particles. Layers of sediment build up over time.

Compaction and cementation

As the layers of sediment build up, the pressure on the lower layers increases. The layers are squeezed together. This process is called compaction. The particles of sediment stick to each other. They get cemented together. This is called cementation.

Rock Cycle

Rocks are constantly being formed, worn down and then formed again. This is known as the rock cycle. It takes several millions of years for rocks to change. All three types of rocks can be changed through the rock cycle.

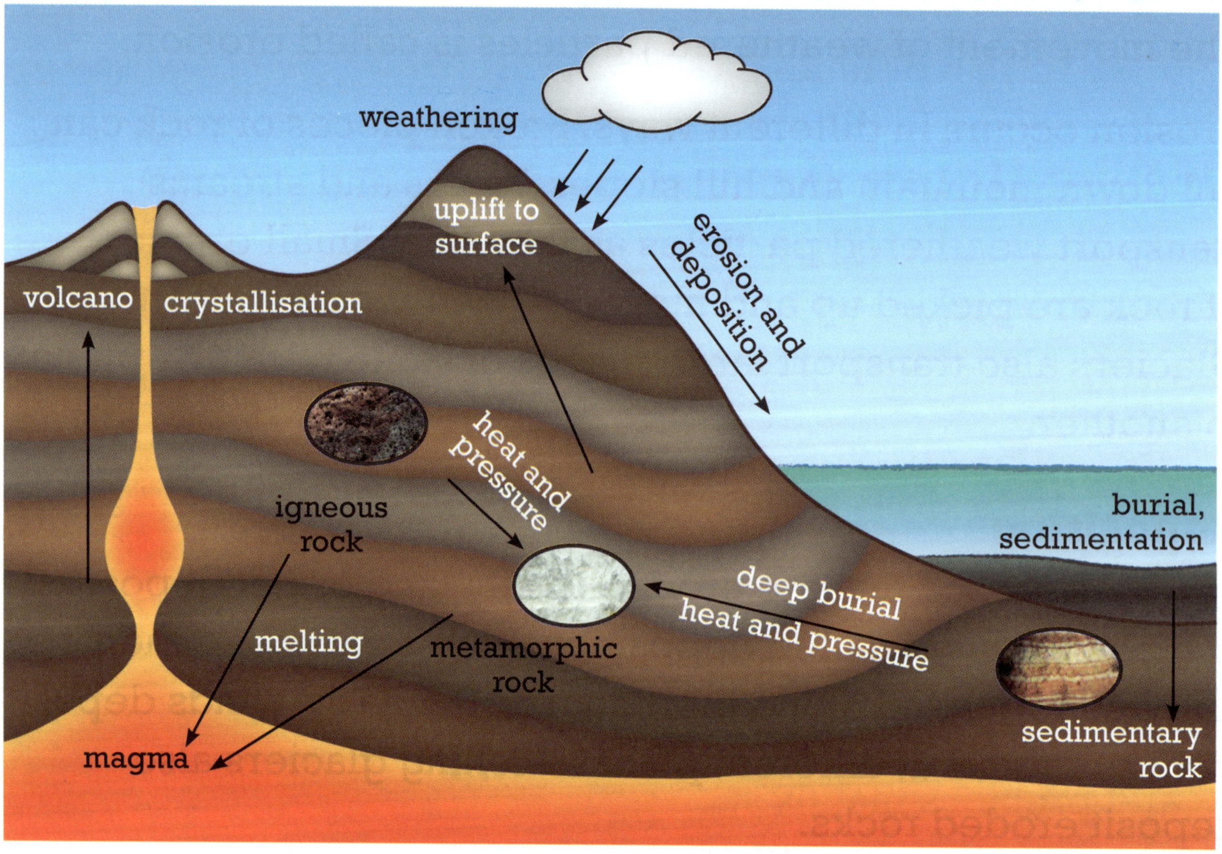

rock cycle — transformation of rocks

 ISBN 978-81-8477-929-5

Minerals

Minerals are the building blocks of rocks. A rock is made up of two or more minerals. Mountains, hills, plains and riverbeds contain minerals.

There are about 4000 different minerals in the world. Silicates are the most common minerals found on the Earth. Salts, talc, metal ores, calcite, magnesium, mica and gemstones are examples of minerals.

Characteristics of Minerals

- They occur naturally.
- They are inorganic, that is, they are made up of non-living matter.
- They are in the solid state of matter.
- They have a definite chemical composition.
- They have a definite internal structure.

Uses of Rocks and Minerals

Rocks and minerals are used for different purposes, some of which are mentioned below.

- Many rocks and minerals are used to make buildings.
- Stone and concrete are used in building roads, highways, tunnels, bridges and airports.
- Many rocks and minerals are used for making beautiful, decorative items.
- Tools are made of metals, which are derived from minerals.
- Jewellery is made from precious or semi-precious stones and precious metals such as gold, silver and platinum.

 ISBN 978-81-8477-929-5

Soil

Soil is one of the most important natural resources on the Earth. It makes up the topmost layer of the surface of the Earth. Soil is a mixture of rocks, minerals and dead, decaying plants and animals. The composition and nature of soil varies from place to place. It is of vital importance to plants, animals and humans. Plants use the nutrients in the soil to live and grow. They anchor their roots in the soil. Soil also provides a home to animals such as insects, centipedes and worms. Some animals dig burrows in soil to keep safe. Human beings depend on soil to grow food.

A study of the layers of the soil reveals three distinct layers or horizons of soil.

Topsoil is the uppermost layer of the soil. It is nearest to the surface. The topsoil is generally dark brown or black in colour. It is made up of rock particles along with organic materials such as dead plants, especially their roots. Decaying matter makes the soil thick and rich. The topsoil is generally full of plant and animal life.

layers of the soil

The **subsoil** consists of rock particle. The proportion of plant life and living organisms in this layer is very low.

  ISBN 978-81-8477-929-5

The **bedrock** consists of large pieces of rock and is usually very deep inside the Earth.

Quiz Time

1. Answer the questions.

a. How many types of rocks are there? Explain each type briefly.

b. What are minerals?

c. Name four commonly found minerals.

d. How do rocks change?

e. Explain the formation of soil in a hundred words. Support your answer with an illustration.

f. What are the different features of igneous, sedimentary and metamorphic rocks? Give two examples of each.

2. Fill in the blanks to complete the sentences.

a. When magma cools and hardens, it turns into ____________________ rock.

b. The movement of weathered particles is called ____________________.

c. A mixture of clay, sand, silt and organic matter makes up ____________________.

d. Acid rain causes ____________________ of rocks.

 ISBN 978-81-8477-929-5

3. Indicate whether the following statements are true (T) or false (F).

a. Sedimentary rocks often have fossils in them. ☐

b. A mineral is a naturally occurring solid substance. ☐

c. The nature of soil is constantly changing. ☐

d. There is a lot of water and air circulating through bedrock. ☐

4. Tick (✓) the correct answer.

a.	Melted rock above ground	☐ lava ☐ magma
b.	Melted rock below ground	☐ lava ☐ magma
c.	Rock formed from magma or lava when it cools	☐ sedimentary ☐ metamorphic ☐ igneous
d.	Rock formed when sediments are pressed or cemented together	☐ sedimentary ☐ metamorphic ☐ igneous
e.	Rock formed from existing rock when the temperature or pressure changes	☐ sedimentary ☐ metamorphic ☐ igneous
f.	Conglomerate	☐ sedimentary ☐ metamorphic ☐ igneous

 ISBN 978-81-8477-929-5

g.	Gneiss	☐ sedimentary ☐ metamorphic ☐ igneous
h.	Granite	☐ sedimentary ☐ metamorphic ☐ igneous
i.	Gypsum	☐ sedimentary ☐ metamorphic ☐ igneous
j.	Limestone	☐ sedimentary ☐ metamorphic ☐ igneous

Can you make diamonds out of coal?

 ISBN 978-81-8477-929-5

8

FORCE

Force is a pull or a push. Objects at rest will not move unless a force acts upon them. For example, a cricket ball will stay at rest unless we pick it up and throw it. Force is necessary to make an object start moving, speed it up, slow it down, stop it from moving, or change its direction.

Force only exists as a result of contact between objects. When the contact ceases, force also ceases to exist.

Forces usually act in a particular direction and in pairs. Hence, if one object exerts force on another object then the other object will exert equal force back on the first object.

Learn More

Add arrows to show the directions of the forces exerted by the objects below.

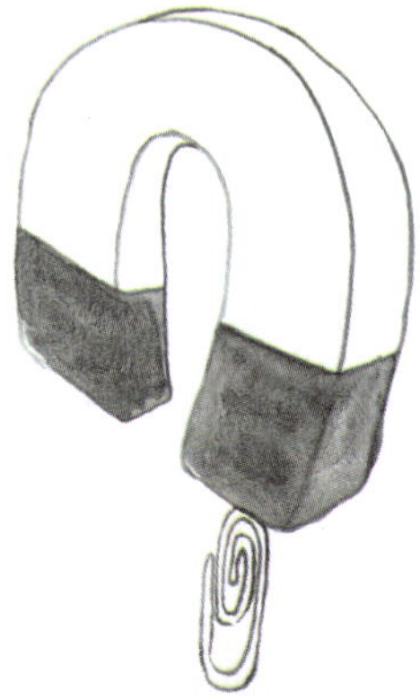

ISBN 978-81-8477-929-5

Types of Forces

Gravity

The force of gravity is the force of attraction between all objects. It tends to pull objects towards one another. Gravity controls the movement of objects in space. It keeps the Moon in orbit around the Earth. It keeps the Earth and other planets of the solar system in orbit around the Sun.

The more mass or volume each object has, the greater the force of attraction. As the distance between the objects increases, the attraction decreases.

When we bike uphill, Earth's gravity pulls us down the hill. Gravity makes it difficult to bike uphill. When we are biking downhill, the Earth's gravity pulls us down, making it easier to cycle.

Circle Time

Why do objects weigh less on the Moon than they do on Earth? Discuss with the rest of the class.

Flotation

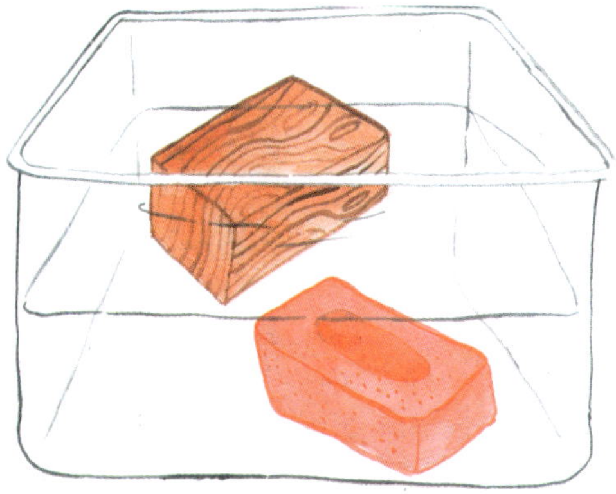

What will happen if we drop a cork and a pebble in a bowl of water? The pebble will sink while the cork will float. Archimedes, an ancient Greek scientist, was the first to study upthrust. He discovered that upthrust was equal to the amount of water displaced. **Upthrust** is the force that pushes an object up such that it appears to

 ISBN 978-81-8477-929-5

lose weight in a liquid or gas. Upthrust is equal to the amount of water displaced. When held under water, two objects of the same size (for example, a brick and a block of wood) will displace the same amount of water. The upthrust in each case is the same. As the brick is heavier, its upthrust is less than its weight and so it sinks. The upthrust on the block of wood is greater than its weight, so it floats.

The **density** of a substance determines whether it will float or sink. Density is the weight of a substance divided by its volume. Oil floats on water because it is less dense than water. Objects have a tendency to float when placed in a fluid. This is called **buoyancy.** Fluids, such as air or water, apply an upward force on objects that are partially or totally submerged in them.

When a person jumps in a pool of water, some of the water splashes up. The person pushes down on the water and the water exerts an upthrust. This causes the splash.

Upthrust or buoyancy, acts not only in liquids but also in gases. This is the reason why an airship filled with helium floats up in the sky. Helium has a lower density than air.

An airship filled with helium floats because the upthrust of the air is greater than its weight.

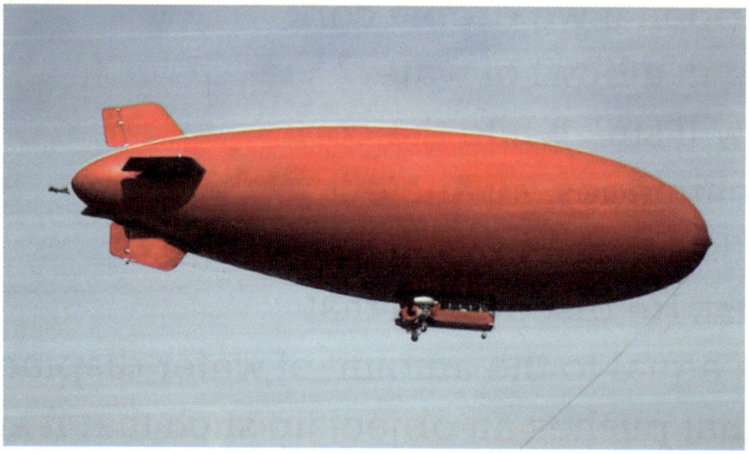

 ISBN 978-81-8477-929-5

Learn More

Investigate how ships made of steel and weighing hundreds of tonnes can float on water.

PRESSURE

Pressure is the force acting on a certain area. Stand with both feet on the floor. Notice that pressure is being exerted through both feet on to the floor. As you stand on one foot, the pressure exerted by one foot will be greater. This is because the force of the body weight is concentrated on to a smaller area. Hence, pressure depends on force (or weight) and the area on which the force is acting.

The motor in a vacuum cleaner drives a fan that forces air out of one end. This creates an area of low air pressure inside the vacuum cleaner. The higher atmospheric pressure outside the vacuum cleaner pushes air into the nozzle, and this air carries dirt and dust with it into the dust bag.

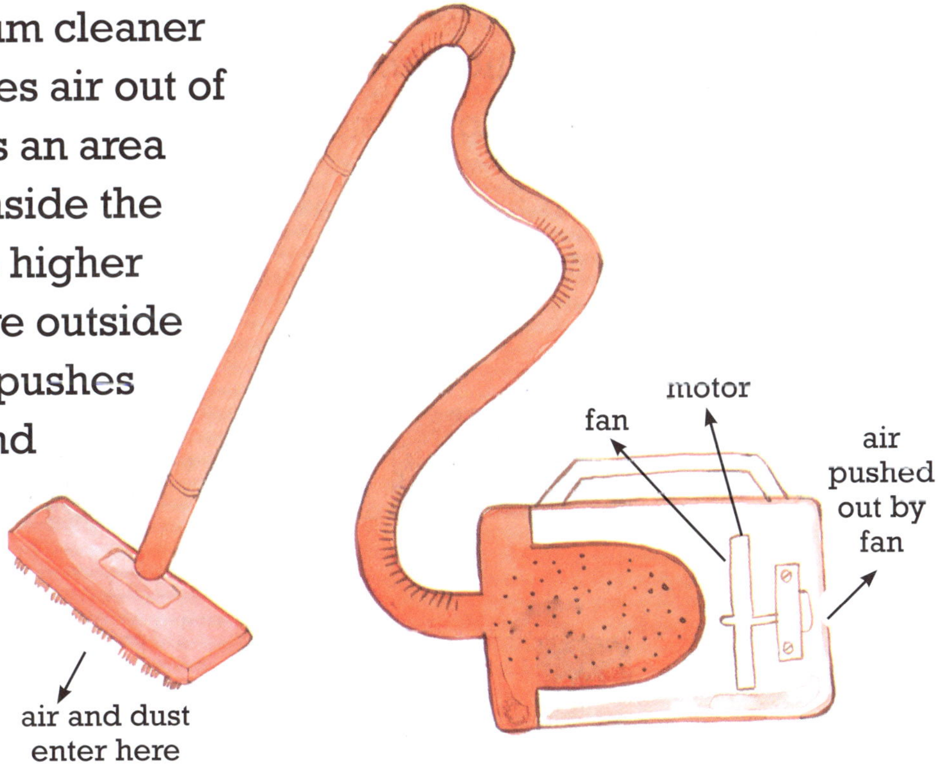

A sharp knife cuts better than a blunt one because the cutting edge has a smaller area, so the pressure it can exert is increased.

 ISBN 978-81-8477-929-5

Magnets

> **Factastic**
> The word magnet comes from Magnesia, a district in Thessaly, Greece.

The ancient Greeks and Chinese discovered that certain rare stones, known as lodestones, were naturally magnetised. These stones could mysteriously attract small pieces of iron towards them. Lodestones always pointed in the same direction when suspended by a piece of string. Magnets have two forces—push and pull. They attract other magnetic objects such as iron and steel. A magnet can influence other magnets or magnetic materials in the area around it. Scientists call this a **field of force** or **magnetic field**.

The ends of a magnet are known as its poles. Each magnet has two poles—North Pole and South Pole. The magnetic effect is the strongest at the poles. Magnetic force is exerted by magnets on each other and on some metals such as iron and nickel.

The poles of a magnet always come in pairs. If we take a bar magnet and break it into two, each piece will again have its

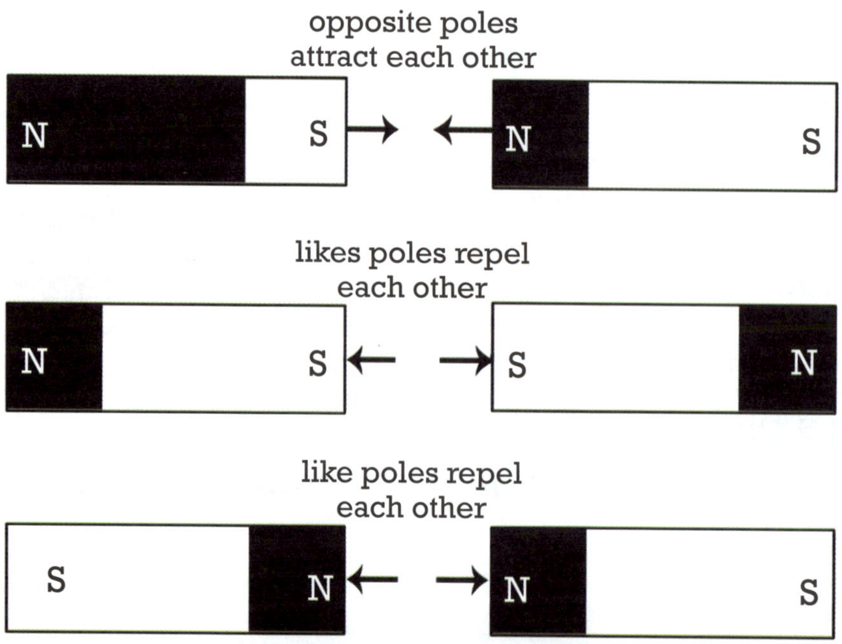

 ISBN 978-81-8477-929-5

own north and south poles. If these pieces are broken down further, each of these smaller pieces too will have their own north and south poles. Hence, no matter how small the pieces of the magnet become, each piece will always have a north pole and a south pole.

Circle Time

Work in groups with a few magnets of various shapes and sizes. Observe and record what happens when the magnets are placed near certain objects and near each other. Also make a list of objects attracted by magnets.

As we place two magnets with their north poles facing each other, the magnets repel, that is, they move away from one another. When the opposite poles are brought face to face, they attract each other.

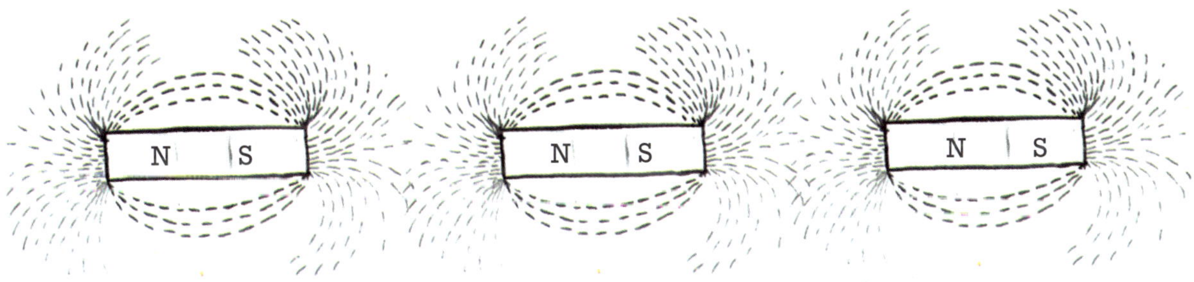

Iron fillings arrange themselves in lines between the poles of a magnet. These are known as magnetic lines of force.

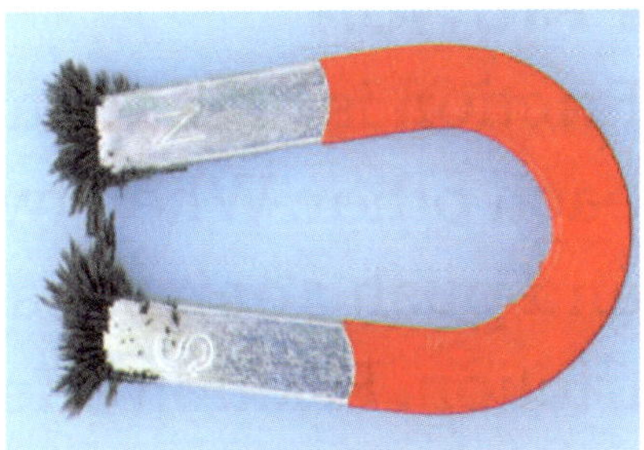

 ISBN 978-81-8477-929-5

The Earth also has a magnetic field. The needle of a compass is a small magnet which aligns itself with the magnetic field of the Earth, so that one end of the needle points to the Earth's magnetic north.

Electromagnetism

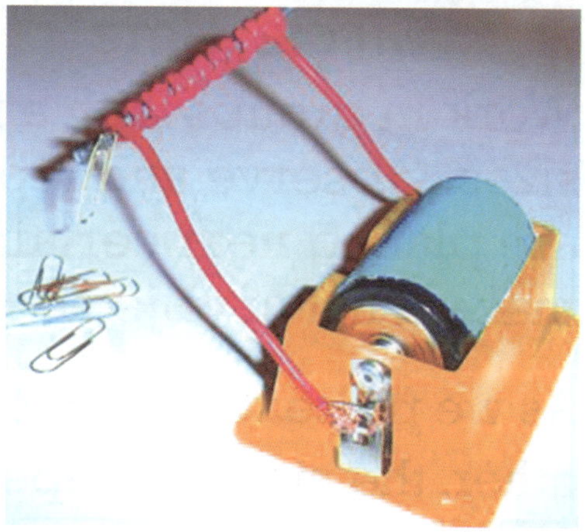

The interaction between electric currents or fields and magnetic fields is known as electromagnetism. A wire coil that has an electric current running through it produces a magnetic field. A nail that is inserted into the coil becomes magnetised. The nail only stays magnetised while the current is flowing. The more the nail turns in the coil, and the greater the current used, the stronger the magnetic field will be.

Electrostatic force is produced by electric charges. Rub a balloon against your hair and then bring it close to tiny bits of paper. The pieces of paper will immediately get attracted towards the balloon. This is because of the electrostatic forces created as we rub the balloon against our hair.

Friction

Friction is created as a result of two objects rubbing against each other. When two objects slide over each other they rub and push against each other. This pushing force is called friction. Friction affects the speed of an object, but not the direction. It acts to slow down a moving object.

 ISBN 978-81-8477-929-5

Friction depends on the surfaces of the objects. When the surfaces are rough, there is more friction. When the objects have smooth surfaces, there will be less friction.

Frictional forces are present all around us. Friction allows people to walk without slipping. Friction helps stop moving cars and bicycles. Sometimes it becomes necessary to increase or decrease the amount of friction. Tyres have grooves and bumps on them. They increase the friction between the tyres and the road. Too much friction can cause rubbing parts in machines to wear out. They can rotate more easily with less friction. People apply oil on machine parts to decrease friction.

Quiz Time

1. Answer the questions.

a. Why are some balloons able to float in air?

b. What is density?

c. Discuss the unique property of magnets.

d. Explain the terms—buoyancy and pressure?

e. What is magnetism? How is it different from electromagnetism?

f. Why is it sometimes necessary to increase or decrease the amount of friction?

g. Explain how gravity keeps the Earth in orbit around the Sun.

 ISBN 978-81-8477-929-5

2. Draw a map of your school and the school playground. Use a compass to mark the cardinal directions on your map.

3. Fill in the blanks with the correct words from the brackets.

a. Upthrust pushes objects up and makes them appear to ________________ weight. (lose/gain/stabilise)

b. Pressure is ________________ acting on a certain area. (friction/gravity/force)

c. People apply oil on machine parts to ________________ friction. (stabilise/increase/decrease)

d. Temporary magnets that work with ________________ are called electromagnets. (friction/gravity/electricity)

4. Indicate whether the following statements are true (T) or false (F).

a. A force can make a moving object change direction. ☐

b. Things at rest will start moving by themselves. ☐

c. The wind and water both exert forces to start or stop things moving. ☐

d. Objects have to touch a magnet to be attracted by it. ☐

e. Opposite poles attract each other. ☐

How do airplanes stay up in the air?

 ISBN 978-81-8477-929-5

9
Energy and Work

The word **energy** means the capacity to do some work. For example, a light bulb will be lit up when it is provided with electricity that is a form of energy. Also, when a river flows with great speed, it exerts force and possesses energy to do some work. Similarly, the muscles in our arms have the ability to lift things. They contain energy, which is used when the muscles work. We can, thus, define energy as the ability to do work.

Energy cannot be created or destroyed. Different forms of energy can, however, be changed from one kind to another. A car's engine burns fuel, converting the chemical energy in fuel into mechanical energy. Solar cells change light energy into electrical energy. In this way, the total amount of energy in the universe stays the same. It can be transferred from one thing to another or from one form to another. For example, a car colliding with another car at rest makes the second car move.

Types of Energy

Mechanical Energy

Mechanical energy is the energy possessed by an object due to its motion or due to its position. Mechanical energy can be of two types—**kinetic energy** (energy of motion) or **potential energy** (stored energy of position).

 ISBN 978-81-8477-929-5

Heat Energy

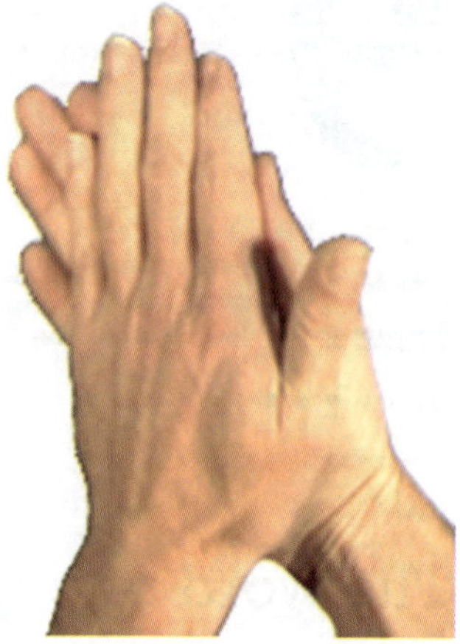

Heat energy is the internal energy in substances generated by the movement of atoms and molecules in substances. Heat energy is also called **thermal energy**. Heat is a form of energy that we get from the Sun and when we burn wood, kerosene and other fuels. It is used for cooking, heating water as well as to keep us warm. When we rub our palms together, heat energy is generated due to friction.

> **Factastic**
> When an object gains energy, it becomes hotter. Similarly, as the object loses energy, it cools down.

Radiant energy is a kind of energy that travels in waves. Radiant energy includes visible light, x-rays, gamma rays and radio waves. Light is one type of radiant energy. Solar energy is also an example of radiant energy.

Light Energy

Light is a special type of energy that is very important. The largest and the most important source of light on Earth is the Sun. Without it we would be unable to see and green plants would be unable to make their own food.

Objects such as the Sun, stars and electric bulbs, give off their own light, which is known as **incandescent** or **direct light**. They radiate light because they are very hot. When direct light from one object is bounced off another object, it is known as **reflected light**. For example, the Moon reflects the light from the Sun.

 ISBN 978-81-8477-929-5

Circle Time

With the help of a mirror, see how light is reflected. What makes a mirror a good reflector?

Not all surfaces reflect light. Light passes through some objects instead of bouncing off them. Materials that allow light to pass through them are known as **transparent materials**. Glass is a good example of a transparent material. Materials that do not allow light to pass through them are known as **opaque materials**. **Translucent materials**, such as butter paper, allow less light to pass through them.

Sound Energy

Sounds we hear are produced by air vibrating. For example, hitting a ruler against a tabletop, or plucking a taut rubber band. As we make an object move or vibrate, it makes a sound. The energy of the vibration is passed on to the tiny molecules of air surrounding the object and makes them move. The stronger the vibration, the louder the sound will be.

The vibrations moving through air are known as **sound waves**. It is when sound waves reach our ears that we hear sound. Sound can only travel through matter. It cannot travel in a vacuum where there is no matter or in outer space.

Sound moves at a speed of about 330 m per second, and can travel through gases, liquids and solids.

Sound levels

The loudness of a sound is measured in decibels (dB).

 ISBN 978-81-8477-929-5

A sound of zero decibels is too low for a human ear to hear and a sound of more than 140 decibels can damage the unprotected ear.

When sound hits a barrier, such as a wall or a cliff, it can be reflected. This is known as an **echo**.

Some sounds along with their levels of loudness are shown in the table.

sound	decibels (dB)
Aircraft engine 	100–200
Jackhammer 	100
Heavy traffic 	90
Conversation 	40-60
Whisper 	20
Leaves rustling 	10

 ISBN 978-81-8477-929-5

Potential Energy

Potential energy is the energy stored in an object due to its position.

> **Factastic**
> Some substances, such as wool, wood and glass are poor conductors of sound and it is for this reason that they are often used to soundproof rooms. The science of sound is known as acoustics.

Chemical Energy

Chemical energy is energy stored in the bonds of atoms and molecules. It is the energy that holds these particles together. Biomass, petroleum, natural gas and propane are examples of stored chemical energy.

We consume carbohydrates as food. Carbohydrate molecules store energy in their atomic bonds. Body cells release this stored energy by a process called respiration. Some of the stored potential energy becomes the kinetic energy of cell functions and muscle movement. Some of it becomes internal heat energy that keeps the body warm.

Nuclear Energy

Nuclear energy is energy stored in the nucleus of an atom. The energy can be released when nuclei are combined or split apart. Nuclear power plants split the nuclei of uranium atoms in a process called **fission**. The Sun combines the nuclei of hydrogen atoms in a process called **fusion**.

Gravitational Energy

Gravitational energy is the energy of position or place. A rock resting at the top of a hill contains potential gravitational energy. Hydropower, such as water in a dam reservoir, is also an example of potential gravitational energy.

ISBN 978-81-8477-929-5

ELECTRICAL ENERGY

atom

Electrical energy is the movement of electrical charges. Everything is made of tiny particles called **atoms**. Atoms are made of even smaller particles called electrons, protons and neutrons. The protons and neutrons are packed in a small sphere in the middle of the atom, called the nucleus. The electrons orbit around the nucleus. Protons and electrons have electrical charges. Protons have a positive charge and electrons have a negative charge. Neutrons have no charge.

When a force is applied, some of the electrons move out of an atom. They hop from atom to atom. The moving electrons contain kinetic energy.

Electrical charges or electrical energy moving through a wire is called **electricity**. Lightning is also an example of electrical energy. We use electricity every day for heat, light and power. Electricity is a form of energy and not an energy source. Electricity can be produced using solar energy, wind, petrol, coal, water, oil, natural gas and chemicals. The electricity we use everyday in our homes moves along wires in what is known as a **current**. Materials that allow electricity to flow through them are called **conductors**. Copper and silver are good conductors of electricity. Materials that do not allow electricity to flow through them are called **insulators**. Rubber and wood are insulators.

 ISBN 978-81-8477-929-5

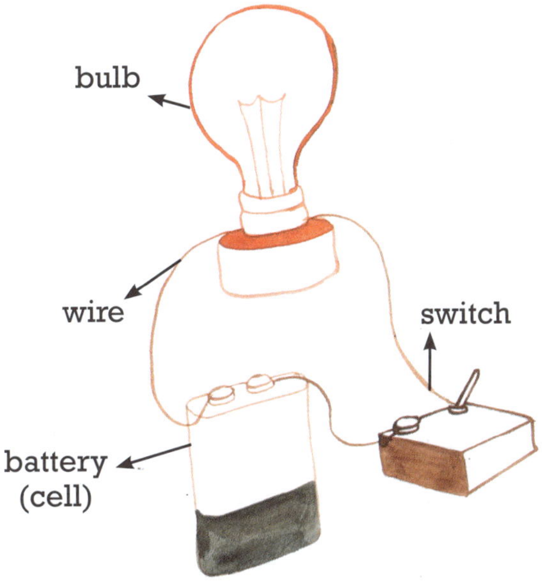

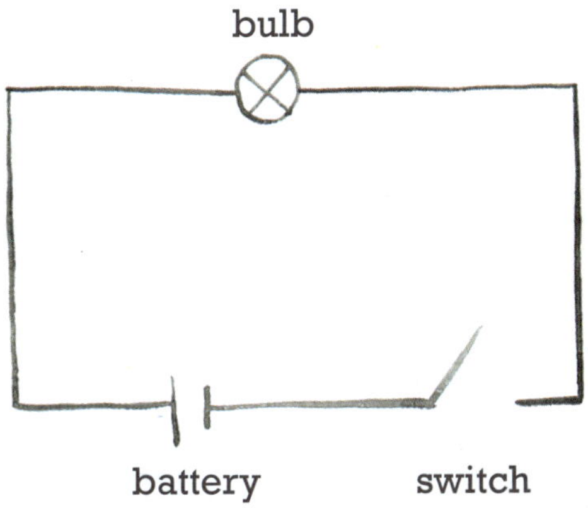

simple electrical circuit

This picture shows a simple electric circuit. A bulb is connected with wires to a battery and a switch. When the switch is turned on, the connection is complete and the bulb lights up. We usually draw a circuit with symbols.

Explore

Study these electrical circuit diagrams. Draw pictures of what they would really look like. Label the components in each picture.

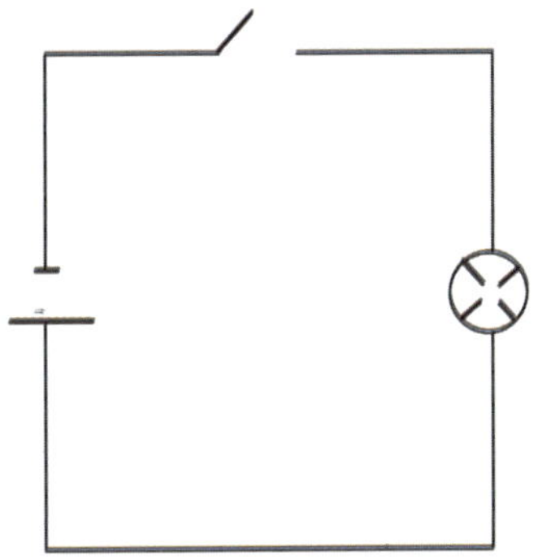

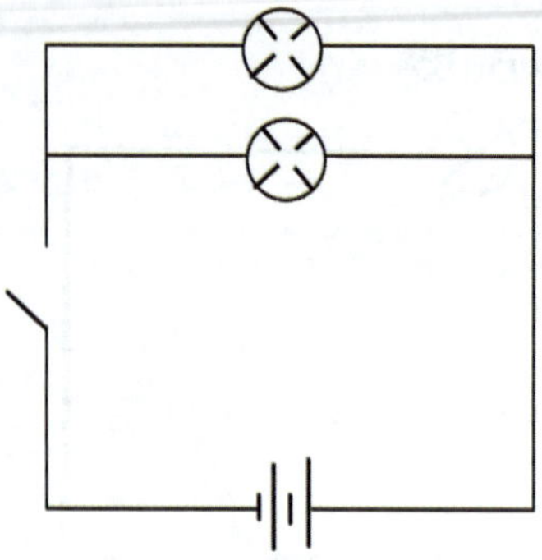

Draw the circuit diagram for this picture.

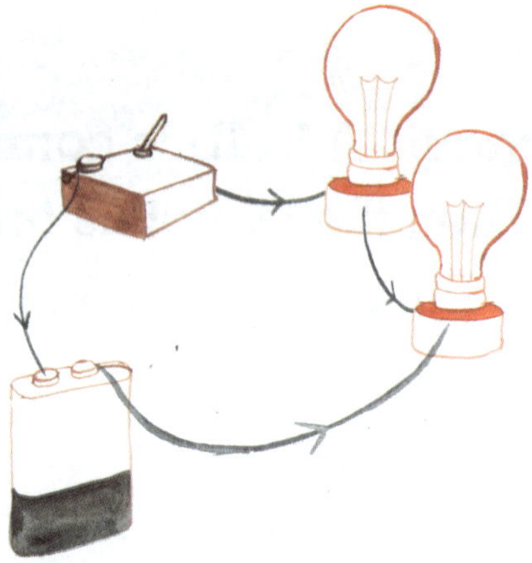

Work

Work is the application of force over a distance. Work is said to be done if the force applied on an object makes the object move in the direction of the force. Work is done when a force applied on an object makes the object move across a distance. The object moves in the direction of the force. Pushing, pulling and lifting are different forms of work.

Simple Machines

Simple machines make work easier for us. They allow us to overcome a force at one place by enabling the force to be applied elsewhere. There are six simple machines—inclined

 ISBN 978-81-8477-929-5

plane, lever, pulley, screw, wedge and the wheel and axle. Complex or compound machines are a combination of two or more simple machines working together.

name	description	how it works and its examples
Inclined plane 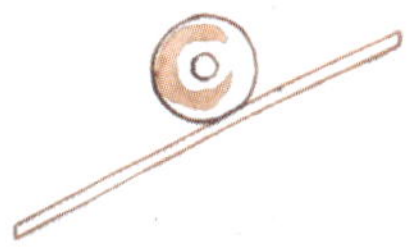	It is a slanting surface connecting a lower level to a higher level	The object moves over a longer distance, but less force is needed since it doesn't have to be lifted up. For example, ramp and a winding uphill road
Lever 	It is a stiff bar that rests on a support known as the fulcrum which lifts or moves loads	The fulcrum can be moved depending on the weight of the object. Pushing down on one end of the lever results in the upward motion of the other end. For example, a see-saw, a bottle opener, a claw
Pulley 	It uses grooved wheels and a rope to raise, lower or move a load	Work is made easier because pulling down on a rope is easier than lifting a weight. For example, a flag pole, blinds
Screw 	It is an inclined plane wrapped around a central axis	It holds things together and/or lifts materials. For example, car jack, a spiral staircase
Wedge 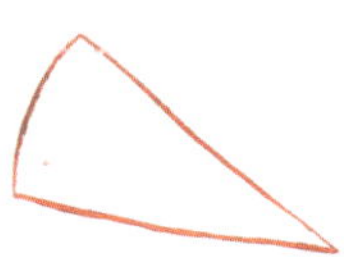	It is an object with at least one slanting side ending in a sharp edge	It is used to cut or split things apart. For example, an axe, a knife
Wheel and axle 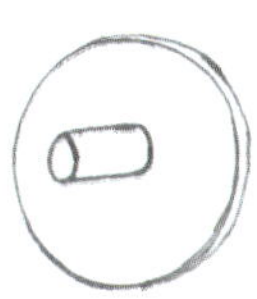	A wheel with a rod (known as the axle)through its centre, lifts or moves loads	As the axle turns, the wheel moves a greater distance, such that less force is needed to move it. For example, a toy car, a door knob

 ISBN 978-81-8477-929-5

Complex Machines

Compound machines are a combination of two or more simple machines working together.

Can opener: The handle that makes the can rotate is a wheel and axle. The two long arms that clamp the can are a lever. The circular wheel that cuts the can's lid has a sharp edge, a wedge.

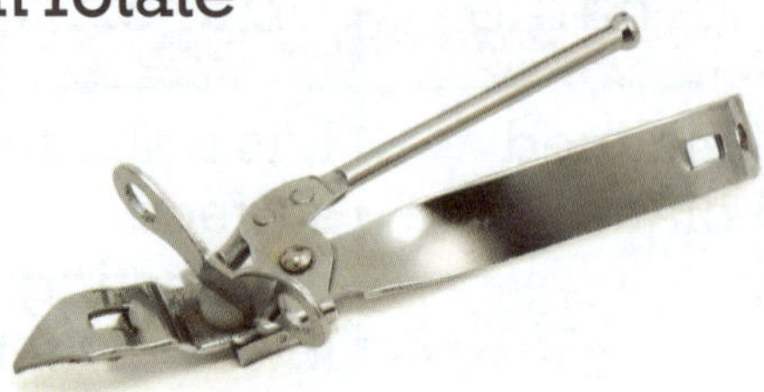

Corkscrew: The handle at the top is a wheel and axle. The spiral metal piece that screws into the cork is a screw. The two side arms that are pushed down are two levers.

Scissors: The two arms of a pair of scissors are levers. The cutting edges of the scissor blades are wedges.

Quiz Time

1. Answer the questions.

a. Explain the relationship between work and force.

b. What is the most important source of light on Earth?

c. Why does a star or a bulb radiate light?

d. What is mechanical energy? Give three examples of mechanical energy.

e. Will sound travel through a vacuum? Why?

f. What are poor conductors of sound used for?

g. What is meant by energy? What is kinetic energy?

 ISBN 978-81-8477-929-5

h. What is the name given to the energy stored in food or petrol?

i. List three things that get their energy from

   i. Electricity

   ii. Wind

   iii. Sunlight

j. Make a list of all the sounds you can hear

   i. In the classroom

   ii. In the playground

2. Indicate whether the following statements are true (T) or false (F).

a.	Light can pass through a transparent object.	☐
b.	Mirrors are the only things that reflect light.	☐
c.	Light is reflected from a mirror because the back of the mirror is covered with silver paint.	☐
d.	An insulator is used to protect electric wires.	☐
e.	When two wires touch each other and sparks occur, it is known as a short circuit.	☐
f.	Copper does not conduct electricity.	☐

3. Fill in the blanks with the correct words from the brackets.

a. A roller skate is an example of a ________________. (lever/wheel and axle/wedge)

b. A see-saw in the play area is an example of a/an ________________. (pulley/lever/inclined plane)

 ISBN 978-81-8477-929-5

c. A fork is an example of a ________________.
(wheel and axle/wedge/pulley)

d. A ramp is an example of a/an ________________.
(screw/wedge/inclined plane)

4. Find and circle the words from the box in the word grid.

conductor wire battery power insulator
filament electron lightning energy

<table>
<tr><td>c</td><td>o</td><td>n</td><td>d</td><td>u</td><td>c</td><td>t</td><td>o</td><td>r</td><td>y</td></tr>
<tr><td>b</td><td>a</td><td>t</td><td>t</td><td>e</td><td>r</td><td>y</td><td>x</td><td>x</td><td>g</td></tr>
<tr><td>i</td><td>n</td><td>s</td><td>u</td><td>l</td><td>a</td><td>t</td><td>o</td><td>r</td><td>r</td></tr>
<tr><td>w</td><td>p</td><td>o</td><td>w</td><td>e</td><td>r</td><td>x</td><td>x</td><td>x</td><td>e</td></tr>
<tr><td>i</td><td>t</td><td>n</td><td>e</td><td>m</td><td>a</td><td>l</td><td>i</td><td>f</td><td>n</td></tr>
<tr><td>r</td><td>e</td><td>l</td><td>e</td><td>c</td><td>t</td><td>r</td><td>o</td><td>n</td><td>e</td></tr>
<tr><td>e</td><td>l</td><td>i</td><td>g</td><td>h</td><td>t</td><td>n</td><td>i</td><td>n</td><td>g</td></tr>
</table>

Why is fire hot?

 ISBN 978-81-8477-929-5

10
AIR AND WATER

The atmosphere is like a blanket that surrounds the Earth. It is divided into five different layers. It is thickest near the surface and thins out with height until it eventually merges with space.

layers of the Earth's atmosphere

The **troposphere** is the first layer just above the surface of the Earth. This is the only layer of the atmosphere where life exists. The troposphere is a thin layer, extending only 14-16 km above the Earth's surface. All weather phenomena like changes in temperature, wind, pressure and moisture occur in this layer.

 ISBN 978-81-8477-929-5

This layer is dense and contains about 80% of the mass of the atmosphere. It is the warmest layer. As we go higher in this layer, the temperature drops. The troposphere is wider at the equator than at the poles.

Earth's weather occurs in the troposphere. The troposphere traps water within the atmosphere as clouds form in this layer.

Energy from the Sun warms the Earth's surface. Most of the heat is radiated. It escapes back into space. Water vapour and carbon dioxide in the troposphere trap some of this heat. This is called the **greenhouse effect**. The greenhouse effect helps keep the Earth warm.

The **tropopause** separates the troposphere from the next layer. The tropopause is called a **cold trap**. Rising water vapour cannot go higher because it changes into ice and is trapped at this level. The tropopause and the troposphere are known as the **lower atmosphere**. The troposphere is the only layer where pollutants collect. The pollutants in the troposphere fall to the ground with rain or are absorbed by the oceans.

The **stratosphere** lies above the troposphere. It extends about 50 km high. This layer of the atmosphere is drier and less dense than the troposphere. The temperature in this layer rises with height due to more absorption of the Sun's ultraviolet radiation.

The stratosphere contains the ozone layer. The ozone absorbs and scatters the Sun's harmful ultraviolet rays. It helps increase the temperature

Factastic

The ozone layer protects us from the harmful ultraviolet rays of the Sun. Ultraviolet rays can cause damage to our skin and eyes, they can damage crops and lead to the melting of polar ice caps and flooding of coastal cities.

 ISBN 978-81-8477-929-5

in the upper portion of the stratosphere. The **stratopause** separates the stratosphere from the next layer.

The **mesosphere** lies above the stratosphere. It extends about 85 km high. The temperature in this layer falls with height. It is the coldest layer of the atmosphere. The cold temperature freezes water vapour forming ice clouds. Meteors from space slow down and burn up upon entering the mesosphere.

The **mesopause** separates the mesosphere from the next layer. The stratosphere and the mesosphere are called the middle atmosphere. The mesosphere has a lower temperature than the stratosphere and is the coldest of all the layers (at -143° C) in the atmosphere.

The **thermosphere** lies above the mesosphere. It extends about 600 km high. There is no definite upper limit to the thermosphere. The temperature rises with height in this layer. The temperatures in this layer can go very high. The air is extremely thin. The International Space Station orbits in this layer, at a height between 320 and 380 km.

The thermosphere is also known as the upper atmosphere. The mesosphere and thermosphere are often referred to together as the **ionosphere**. They reflect the ionized energy of the Sun.

The **exosphere** is the uppermost layer of the atmosphere. It is extremely thin as it merges into space.

Life on Earth is possible from a few kilometers above sea level (airborne organisms and life on mountains) to a few kilometres below sea level.

 ISBN 978-81-8477-929-5

The **biosphere** is the portion of Earth in which all known life forms exist. It occupies a thin layer of air (atmosphere), water (hydrosphere) and land (lithosphere).

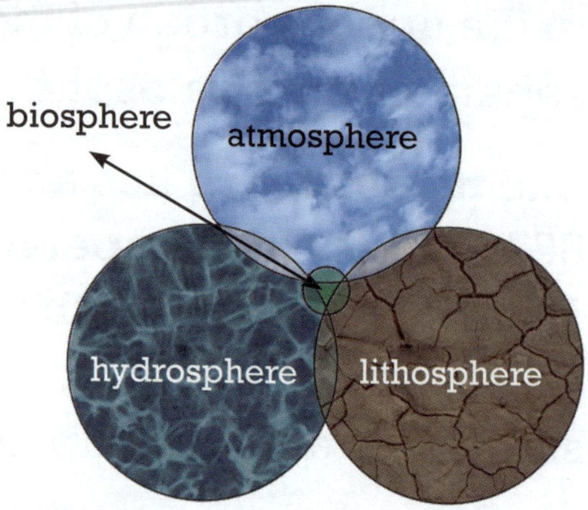

Circle Time

For what reason does the sky becomes suddenly reddish when the Sun sets? Why does this red color only appear during a sunset or sunrise and not when it is noon?

Composition of the Atmosphere

Two gases make up the bulk of the Earth's atmosphere: nitrogen (78%) and oxygen (21%). Argon, carbon dioxide and various trace gases make up the remainder. There are also small particles, or particulates, floating in the atmosphere, such as dust and pollen.

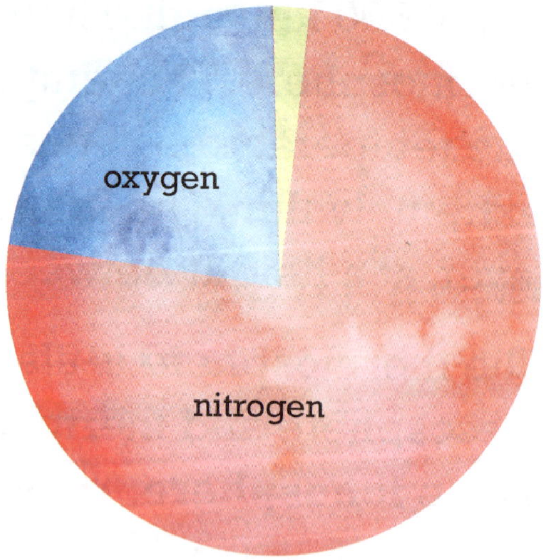

other gases—argon, carbon dioxide and ozone

Living things use nitrogen to make proteins. **Nitrogen** cannot be used directly from the air. Bacteria in the soil convert nitrogen into useable forms. Plant roots absorb this from the soil. Animals depend on plants and other animals to get nitrogen to make proteins.

Oxygen is used by living things for respiration. It is also necessary to burn fuels.

 ISBN 978-81-8477-929-5

Plants use **carbon dioxide** during photosynthesis to make food and release oxygen in the process. Carbon dioxide also absorbs heat and helps keep the Earth warm.

Water vapour in the air comes from evaporation of water from waterbodies. The amount of water vapour in the air varies from place to place. Hot and polar deserts have very little water vapour in the air. The amount of water vapour in the air is called **humidity**.

Air Pressure and Wind

The atmosphere has weight and pushes down on Earth. The constant push of air is called **air pressure**.

Moving air is called **wind**. As the Sun heats the land, the air above also warms up and rises. This creates an area of low pressure. Cold air rushes in to replace the rising air. This movement of air creates winds.

Air warms up over land faster because land retains heat. Over the sea, the air warms up more slowly. This difference causes land and sea breezes.

a sailboat air exerts pressure to make it move forward

During the day, land heats up faster than water in the seas. As the land becomes warmer, it heats the air in the atmosphere above it. This causes the air to expand. It becomes less dense. This creates a low pressure.

 ISBN 978-81-8477-929-5

In comparison, there is a higher pressure over the sea. Wind blows from areas of high pressure towards areas of low pressure. So wind blows from the sea towards the land. This is known as a **sea breeze**.

At night, land cools down much faster than the water. As the land becomes cooler, so does the air above it. The air becomes denser. It forms an area of high pressure. This causes winds to blow from land towards the sea. This is known as a **land breeze**.

Although we cannot see air, we know that it is made up of different types of gases. Air also contains solid particles such as ash and dust. It contains ice crystals and droplets of water. Air has weight, it occupies space and exerts pressure.

a windmill
air pressure makes objects move

air is compressed to be filled into car tyres

tree swaying
moving air is known as wind

an inflated balloon
air occupies space and has weight as well

WATER

Water covers more than two-thirds of the Earth's surface. It is found on the surface, under the surface and in the lower layers of the atmosphere. Water helps regulate the Earth's temperature.

  ISBN 978-81-8477-929-5

It also regulates the temperature of the human body, carries nutrients and oxygen to body cells. It helps in the functioning of the various organs. It makes up large parts of the blood, brain and lungs. Water is essential for plants to produce food. It also helps in the functioning of plant cells. Sap in plants is mainly made up of water.

Most of the water on the Earth is in oceans and trapped as ice. Fresh water represents less than 0.5% of the total water on the Earth.

Of the total percentage of water available, only 3% can actually be used for drinking. The water that is used for drinking comes from rivers, lakes, ponds and wells, which is usually mixed with impurities such as sand, mud and germs. Besides drinking and cooking, people use water for agriculture, power generation and in industries.

In order to make water fit for consumption, it has to be purified. There are two kinds of impurities in water—insoluble and soluble impurities. **Soluble impurities**, such as salt and sugar, may completely dissolve in water. **Insoluble impurities**, such as sand, clay and organic matter, can be removed by allowing the water to stand and draining out the clear portions by filtration or sedimentation.

Purification of Water

In order to purify water and make it fit for drinking, we can either boil or distil it. Apart from this, the addition of chlorine to water helps in killing germs that are not visible to the naked eye. This process of purification is known as **chlorination**.

 ISBN 978-81-8477-929-5

Insoluble impurities such as sand, are separated from water by filtration or sedimentation. In the process of **filtration**, the residue or insoluble part is separated from the filtrate or the solvent using a filter paper.

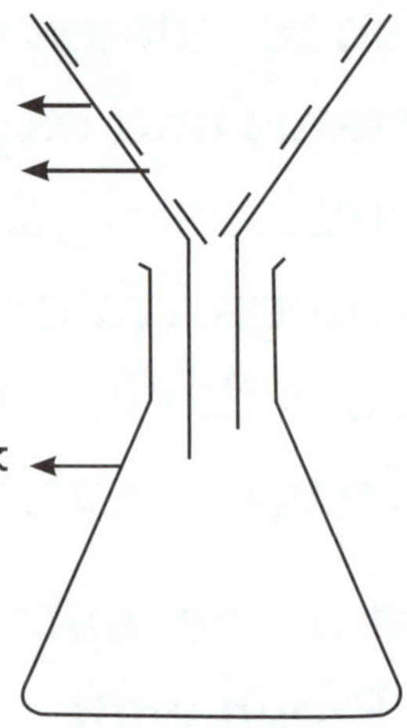

filtration

The insoluble part remains on the filter paper and clean water passes into the beaker.

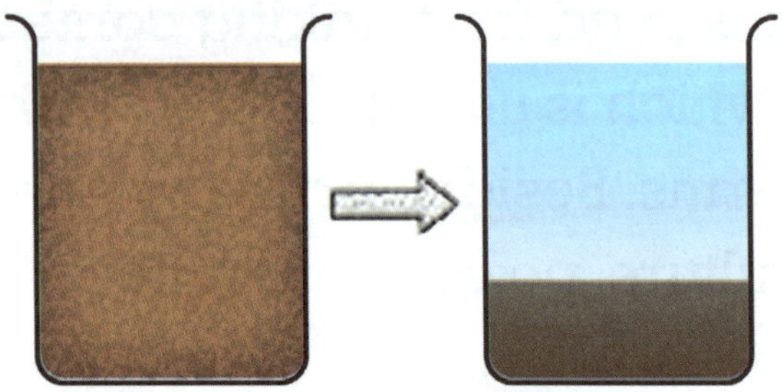
sedimentation

In the process of **sedimentation**, the muddy water is allowed to stand for a while. The mud settles to the bottom and the clean water is decanted into another beaker.

Soluble impurities, such as salt and sugar, are removed using the process of evaporation or distillation.

The process of water turning into water vapour is known as **evaporation**. The salt or sugar water is the solution. Salt is the solute and water is the solvent. When water evaporates, the impurities in the form of salt or sugar are left behind.

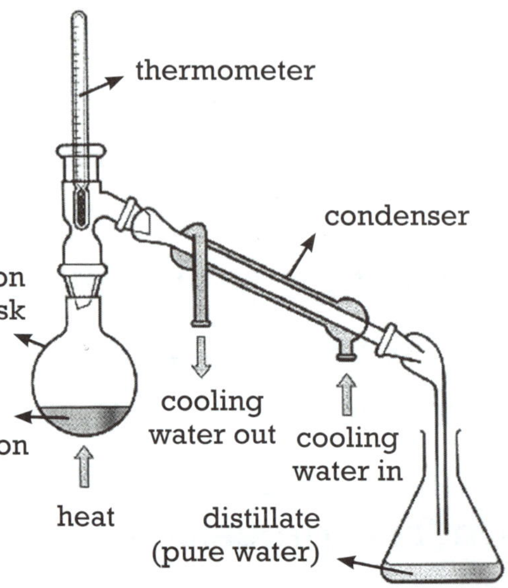

distillation

Distillation is a process of separating impurities from a solution. Pure water is obtained

 ISBN 978-81-8477-929-5

from a mixture of soluble impurities and water using a Liebig condenser. The solution is placed in a round-bottomed flask and heated. Water vapour passes through the long tube of the condenser and cools down and condenses back into water. The pure water is collected in a flask. The impurities remain at the bottom of the round-bottomed flask.

Quiz Time

1. Answer the questions.

a. What is air? Why is it important for us?

b. What are the properties of air?

c. Name the gases which make up the atmosphere.

d. Explain the importance of the atmosphere.

e. Give examples of impurities found in water.

f. How is water purified to make it suitable for drinking?

2. Explain the following with illustrations.

a. Filtration

b. Sedimentation

c. Distillation

3. Fill in the blanks with the correct words from the brackets.

a. The mesosphere lies above the ________________.
(exosphere/stratosphere/atmosphere)

 ISBN 978-81-8477-929-5

b. The ________________ is called a cold trap. (mesosphere/stratopause/tropopause)

c. Oxygen is used by living things for ________________. (photosynthesis/perspiration/respiration)

d. The total quantity of ________________ on the Earth's surface remains the same. (water/food/trees)

4. Indicate whether the following statements are true (T) or false (F).

a. In evaporation, water turns into water vapour. ☐

b. Exosphere is the coldest layer of the atmosphere. ☐

c. Distilled water is the purest form of water. ☐

d. The lower parts of the atmosphere are denser. ☐

How long does it take for a piece of paper to fall to the ground?

 ISBN 978-81-8477-929-5

11
The Solar System

The solar system consists of the Sun, the planets Mercury, Venus, Earth, Mars, Jupiter, Saturn, Uranus and Neptune. It includes the satellites of the planets, dwarf planets, comets, asteroids and meteoroids. Dust and gas are also part of the solar system.

Pluto orbits the Sun beyond the orbit of Neptune. It is much smaller than the planets and is classified as a dwarf planet.

The planets revolve around the Sun. They have nearly circular orbits. The Sun contains 99.85% of the matter in the solar system. The planets make up the remaining mass of the solar system.

Most of the water on the Earth is in oceans and trapped as ice.

 ISBN 978-81-8477-929-5

The eight planets are in constant motion around the Sun. Unlike the Sun, which is a star, the planets do not have any light of their own. The first four planets, namely Mercury, Venus, Earth and Mars are small in size and are mainly made up of rocks. The next four, namely, Jupiter, Saturn, Uranus and Neptune, are giant planets made up of gases.

Learn More

Create your own book on the Sun, Moon and the eight planets. Draw pictures and write about each of them in detail.

Here is the format guidelines for the book.

- There must be a cover page.
- The book must not exceed 12 spreads or 24 pages.
- It must be handwritten.
- Pictures can be drawn or cut-outs can be used.
- References can be used, but not copied.

Information to be included:

- Average distance of the planets from the Sun and the distance from the Earth
- Temperature of the planets
- Diameter of the planets, mass and colour of the planets, number of moons, rings, description of the type of planets and type of terrain
- Duration of a day, a year, orbiting speed of the planets
- Three interesting facts on each planet

 ISBN 978-81-8477-929-5

- Ancient Greeks and Romans, who spotted the planets named them after gods and goddesses. Find out the names of the gods and goddesses associated with the planets. One theory about the beginning of the universe is called the Big Bang theory. Research the Big Bang theory and include it in the project.

Quiz Time

What makes the Earth rotate?

 ISBN 978-81-8477-929-5

12 NATURAL PHENOMENA

Our planet is a peaceful place to live in, but the forces of nature can cause a lot of destruction. Humans have no control over natural phenomena such as volcanoes, earthquakes, tidal waves, floods and storms.

VOLCANOES

Earth has several distinct layers. The outermost layer of the Earth is the **crust**. This comprises the continents and ocean basins. The crust is about 35-70 km thick in the continents and 5-10 km thick in the ocean basins. The next layer is the **mantle** which is about 2900 km thick. The last layer is the **core**, which is separated into the liquid outer core and the solid inner core.

A volcano is an opening in the Earth's crust through which hot molten rock, ash and gases erupt. Molten rock within the Earth's crust is called **magma**. Pressure begins to increase when thick magma and large amounts of gas build up under the Earth's surface. Magma begins to rise slowly through cracks in the crust. The ground above the magma grows as the heated rocks expand. Volcanoes are often found near the boundaries of tectonic plates. These are natural cracks through which the magma erupts. As magma rises, it lets off gases. These gases cause explosions that blow holes called

  ISBN 978-81-8477-929-5

vents or craters at the top of the volcano.

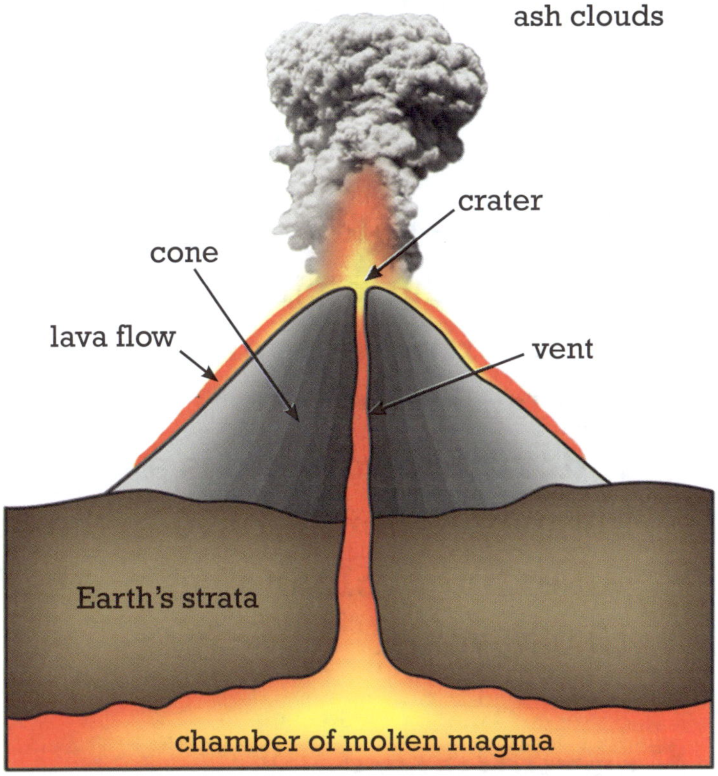

When the magma erupts, it is called **lava**. It flows out like a river. It can be thick and slow-moving or thin and fast-moving. Gases and rock also shoot up through the vents. The lava and rocks that erupt from volcanoes collect and harden around the vent. They build up into mountain-like mounds. This can happen over a period of weeks or many millions of years.

A volcanic eruption can be very dangerous. Hot, flowing lava burns everything in its path. Boulders of hardening lava can crash down on towns and villages. It can cause mudflows from melting snow in mountains. Large parts of towns and cities can get buried. Ash and toxic gases from volcanoes are dangerous to breathe. Volcanoes may also burn and destroy forests. Some erupting volcanoes may trigger floods and earthquakes.

> **Factastic**
> The word 'volcano' is derived from the name of Vulcano island off Sicily which in turn, was named after Vulcan, the Roman god of fire.

Volcanoes have played an important role in the Earth's geological formation. The sea floor, islands and several mountains were formed by volcanic eruptions. Gases from

 ISBN 978-81-8477-929-5

volcanoes formed the Earth's atmosphere. Volcanoes provide valuable mineral deposits that make soil fertile.

Volcanoes are classified according to their level of activity.

- An **active volcano** is a volcano that has had at least one eruption during the past 10,000 years.
- An **intermittent volcano** is a volcano that erupts at regular intervals.
- A **dormant volcano** is a volcano that is currently inactive, but may become active in the future.
- An **extinct volcano** has not had an eruption for at least 10,000 years.

Earthquakes

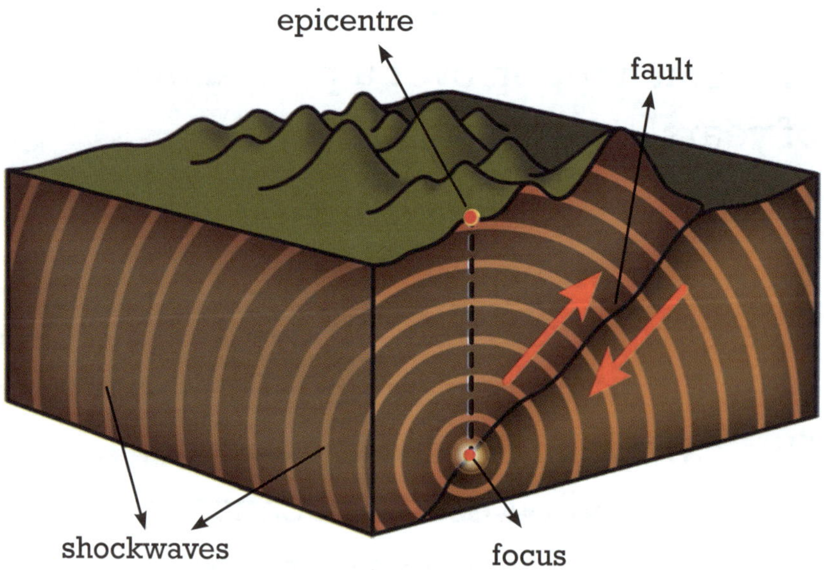

An earthquake is a sudden violent shaking of the ground as a result of movements within the Earth's crust. The Earth's outer shell, the lithosphere, is made of many irregular, rigid segments called **tectonic plates**.

The plates of the crust move constantly as they float on the Earth's mantle. The movement happens extremely slowly. Some plates move at a speed of 15 centimetres per year while others shift at less than 2.5 centimetres per year. The plates can slide past, move away or even bump into each other.

 ISBN 978-81-8477-929-5

When these plates slide against each other, or collide, it results in an earthquake. Most earthquakes occur at depths of less than 80 km from the surface of the Earth.

The point where the earthquake occurs is called the **hypocentre**. It can be hundreds of kilometres below the Earth's surface or just beneath it. The point directly above the hypocentre on the Earth's surface is called the **epicentre**. When the earthquake begins, seismic waves travel outwards in all directions from the hypocentre.

Earthquakes often occur as a series of quakes. **Foreshocks** are smaller earthquakes that are followed by a larger one in the same place. The largest earthquake is called the **mainshock**. Aftershocks are smaller earthquakes that follow the mainshock. Sometimes, aftershocks can continue for weeks, months and even years.

Scientists who study earthquakes are called **seismologists**. They describe earthquakes in terms of their magnitude and intensity. **Magnitude** is a measure of the total energy released during an earthquake. It tells how strong or weak the earthquake was. The **intensity** of an earthquake is a measure of the vibrations created by the earthquake.

The magnitude of earthquakes is measured on the **Richter scale**. The Richter Scale measures earthquakes on a scale of 1 to 10, with 1 being the least powerful and 10 being the most powerful. Little damage is done by an earthquake below 4.0. An earthquake of 7.0 causes widespread destruction.

 ISBN 978-81-8477-929-5

Explore

An earthquake hit the small town of Bhuj in Gujarat a few years ago. Find out the exact location of Bhuj on the map of India. Create a chart on the destruction that the earthquake brought with it.

Factastic

The largest recorded earthquake in the world took place in Chile on 22 May 1960. It had a magnitude 9.5 (Mw).

Circle Time

What happens before and after an earthquake? Discuss.

Tidal Waves

A tidal wave is caused by the gravitational pull of the Moon and the Sun. As the tide rolls in and out, it produces a rise and fall in the sea level. This stretches across thousands of kilometres.

Tidal waves are most evident in narrow bays or in rivers along the coast. As the tide forces its way into these waterbodies, it can raise the water level by several metres in just a few hours. A tidal wave follows the currents. It is a predictable event.

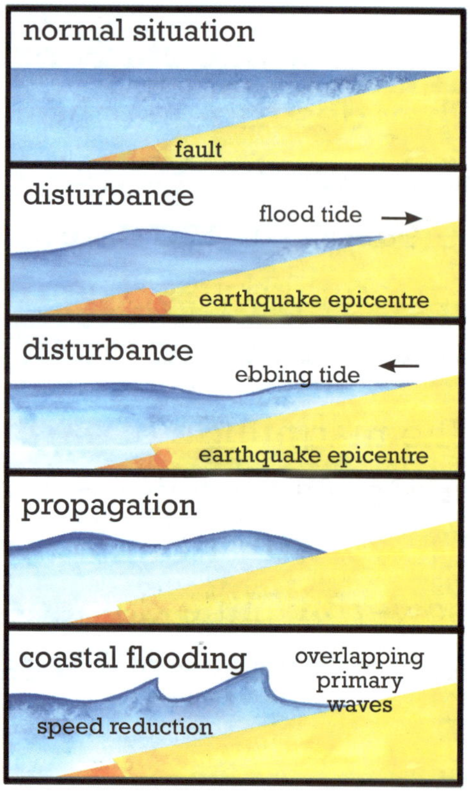

 ISBN 978-81-8477-929-5

A **tsunami** is a series of very high waves in the ocean. It occurs when there is a major disturbance in the ocean. An earthquake or volcanic eruption, for example, can displace the ocean floor and set off an underwater landslide. The water above rises or falls. It creates a series of waves that can travel at hundreds of kilometres an hour. To begin with, the waves are not very tall. They may be hardly noticeable. As they approach land, the water piles up. The resultant waves appear to be giant walls of water. The waves may reach more than 20 metres in height.

Factastic

Tsunami means harbour wave. They cause no visible effect in deep sea, but cause devastation along the coastline.

TORNADO

A **tornado** is a powerful thunderstorm that appears as a rotating, funnel-shaped cloud. The funnel of spiralling winds extends from a thunderstorm to the ground. Twisters are very violent and destructive in nature. They are formed beneath thunderclouds.

tornado

A tornado is also known as a **twister**. A tornado that forms over water is called a **waterspout**. When it forms over a desert, it is called a **dust devil.**

A tornado can spin faster than 400 km per hour and can move as fast as 100 km per hour across land. A tornado finally loses its intensity and scatters.

ISBN 978-81-8477-929-5

Tornadoes are classified based on their strength. A weak tornado has a speed of less than 170 km per hour. It can last up to 10 minutes. About 69% of tornadoes are weak. A strong tornado can have speeds ranging from 170 km per hour to 325 km per hour. It can last for up to 20 minutes. About 29% of tornadoes are strong. A violent tornado occurs rarely. Only 2% of tornadoes are violent. This type of tornado has a speed greater than 320 km per hour and can last for about an hour.

A tornado can cause a lot of destruction with high wind speeds. It leaves a trail of destruction that can be several kilometres wide. It destroys buildings and roads and can uproot trees.

> **Factastic**
> A tornado that struck Kansas, USA, in 1879, tore up an iron bridge and completely dried the river beneath it.

Hurricanes, Cyclones and Typhoons

A **hurricane** is a violent and destructive storm. It develops from warm, moist air over the ocean in the tropics. As the warm, moisture-rich air over the ocean's surface rises, it forms an area of low pressure. Surrounding air rushes in to replace it. This air becomes warm and moisture-rich too. It rises and more surrounding air gets sucked in. The rising air cools and its moisture condenses into clouds.

cyclone

The entire hurricane air system can be several kilometres wide. It spins counter-clockwise in the Northern Hemisphere. It spins clockwise in the Southern Hemisphere. As the system spins

 ISBN 978-81-8477-929-5

faster and faster, a calm area forms at its centre. This is called the hurricane's eye. The eye is usually 30 to 50 km wide.

Hurricanes originate over oceans in certain regions near the Equator. The north Atlantic Ocean experiences many hurricanes. Hurricanes that happen over the Pacific Ocean are called **typhoons**. Hurricanes near Australia and in the Indian Ocean are called **tropical cyclones**.

Hurricanes have several effects. They can cause storm surges. These are rising walls of water that land on the coast. They cause large-scale deaths and destruction on the shore. They also cause high winds with speeds of up to 320 km per hour.

Most hurricanes last between five and seven days. Some can last more than a month before dying out.

Quiz Time

1. Write a short note.

a. Earthquake

b. Active volcano

c. Tornado

d. Hurricane

2. Answer the questions.

a. What is the epicentre of an earthquake?

b. Which area is most affected by a tsunami?

c. How are tectonic plates associated with earthquakes?

d. Explain the formation of a volcano.

 ISBN 978-81-8477-929-5

e. Name two characteristics of a tsunami.

f. What is a hurricane? How does it develop?

3. Find and circle the words in the word grid.

a. Not active and not extinct (7)

b. Storms that appear over the Indian Ocean are known by this name (7)

c. The scale to measure the intensity of an earthquake (7)

d. Another word for strength (9)

e. The focus or location where the earthquake originates underground (10)

f. An opening from where magma erupts (7)

s	x	d	o	r	m	a	n	t	i	h
m	e	y	z	x	w	u	v	x	n	y
a	r	i	c	h	t	e	r	z	t	p
g	b	c	s	u	z	x	p	p	e	o
n	d	e	f	m	q	r	s	t	n	c
i	c	y	c	l	o	n	e	u	s	e
t	b	c	d	k	l	g	w	v	i	n
u	e	f	g	m	n	o	r	x	t	t
d	h	i	j	z	x	y	z	a	y	r
e	v	o	l	c	a	n	o	y	m	e

 ISBN 978-81-8477-929-5

4. Indicate whether the following statements are true (T) or false (F).

a. An earthquake releases a lot of energy. ☐

b. Volcanoes are usually far from the boundaries of tectonic plates. ☐

c. A hurricane air system spins counter-clockwise in the Northern Hemisphere. ☐

d. A tsunami usually forms in a giant thunderstorm called a supercell. ☐

'Uncontrolled blazes fueled by weather, wind and dry underbrush...' Do you know which natural phenomena is being discussed?

 ISBN 978-81-8477-929-5

13

Saving the Environment

Throughout the Earth's history, there have been changes in its climate. There have been cold and hot periods. This is called climate change. Climate change can be a natural process. However, some scientists believe that over the last two centuries, climate change has been taking place rapidly. Human activities have been blamed for the speed at which this change has occurred.

Pollution

Harmful changes that occur in the environment due to human activities is pollution. Pollution could be of air, water or land. Air pollution affects the air, water pollution affects the water and marine life, and land pollution affects the land destroying life and the environment. There is also another type of pollution known as noise pollution, which is caused by loud noises and sounds. All kinds of pollution are gradually destroying our planet.

Air pollution

The addition of harmful pollutants in the air causes air pollution. Air pollution can have natural or human causes.

Volcanoes are one of the biggest causes of natural air pollution. They spread a large amount of ash in the air. Dust storms are

ISBN 978-81-8477-929-5

another type of natural pollution. The wind blows dirt and sand into the atmosphere. Forest fires spread smoke across large distances.

Industries and different forms of transportation contribute to air pollution all around the world. Vehicles, factories and power plants release chemicals, gases, smoke and soot into the atmosphere. Cities with a lot of traffic and industries are often covered with smog. Smog is a mix of smoke, gases and moisture.

Some pollutants in the atmosphere fall back on the Earth as acid rain. This happens when they combine with moisture in clouds. The mixture produces acidic rain, snow, hail or fog. Acidic precipitation damages plants. It poisons the soil, rivers, lakes and streams. It also destroys forests and wildlife.

Water pollution

When pollutants enter lakes, streams, rivers, oceans, and other waterbodies, they cause water pollution. Some pollutants dissolve in water while others float or get deposited at the bottom of waterbodies. Polluted water is toxic for aquatic plants and animals. Several pollutants seep down into the ground and pollute groundwater.

A large amount of sewage ends up in waterbodies. Household waste contains chemicals from soaps, washing powders and household cleaning agents. When wastes from farms and industries enter rivers, lakes and streams, they cause extensive pollution. Such water can have many toxic chemicals and carries disease-causing germs.

 ISBN 978-81-8477-929-5

Sometimes there are oil spills at sea. The oil that spills from tankers and ships pollutes ocean water. Oil does not dissolve in water and forms a thick layer on the water's surface. It blocks out sunlight and air for aquatic plants and animals. It is poisonous for aquatic life.

Land pollution

Land pollution is caused by dumping of waste matter, mining and harmful agricultural practices.

Soil gets polluted by the overuse of fertilisers, pesticides and insecticides. Soil also gets polluted when industrial chemicals and household wastes are dumped into the ground. Household waste, such as plastics, glass and metal waste do not decay quickly. They pile up and clog the soil.

Effects of Pollution

The Earth's atmosphere contains gases such as carbon dioxide, methane, ozone, water vapour and nitrous oxide in trace amounts. They are known as greenhouse gases. They help regulate the Earth's temperature by trapping heat within the atmosphere. They shield the Earth from the harmful ultraviolet rays of the Sun.

But over the last few decades, the temperature of the Earth has been changing. It is becoming warmer than usual. This is known as **global warming**.

People burn fossil fuels to make power and to run vehicles and machines. When fossil fuels are burned, they release greenhouse gases. These gases escape into the atmosphere.

 ISBN 978-81-8477-929-5

Over the past two centuries, human activities have been releasing more and more of greenhouse gases into the atmosphere. The levels of methane and nitrous oxide in the air have risen because of extensive farming practices. Some industries release gases such as chlorofluorocarbons (CFCs). These harm the ozone layer in the atmosphere.

Over the years, many of Earth's forests have been cut down for wood or cleared for farmland and homes. This has worsened the balance of carbon dioxide in the air. When forests are cleared, the carbon stored in the trees escapes as carbon dioxide into the atmosphere. As a result, the amount of carbon dioxide in the air is continuing to increase.

With more greenhouse gases in the air, the Earth is becoming warmer. As a result, Earth's climate is changing. **Carbon footprint** is a measure of the impact of human activities on the Earth's environment. It takes into account the amount of greenhouse gases produced through burning fossil fuels for electricity, heating and transportation.

Another man-made cause of global warming is the increasing population.

If the Earth keeps on getting warmer and warmer, some plants and animals may eventually become extinct forever.

There can be several outcomes of global warming.

- Some heat-tolerant species may evolve.
- Cooler places may become hotter and drier.
- Lakes and rivers may shrink. New coastlines may form and coastal cities may get flooded.

 ISBN 978-81-8477-929-5

- Forests could disappear.
- Hurricanes, tsunamis and tidal waves could become more frequent and more intense.

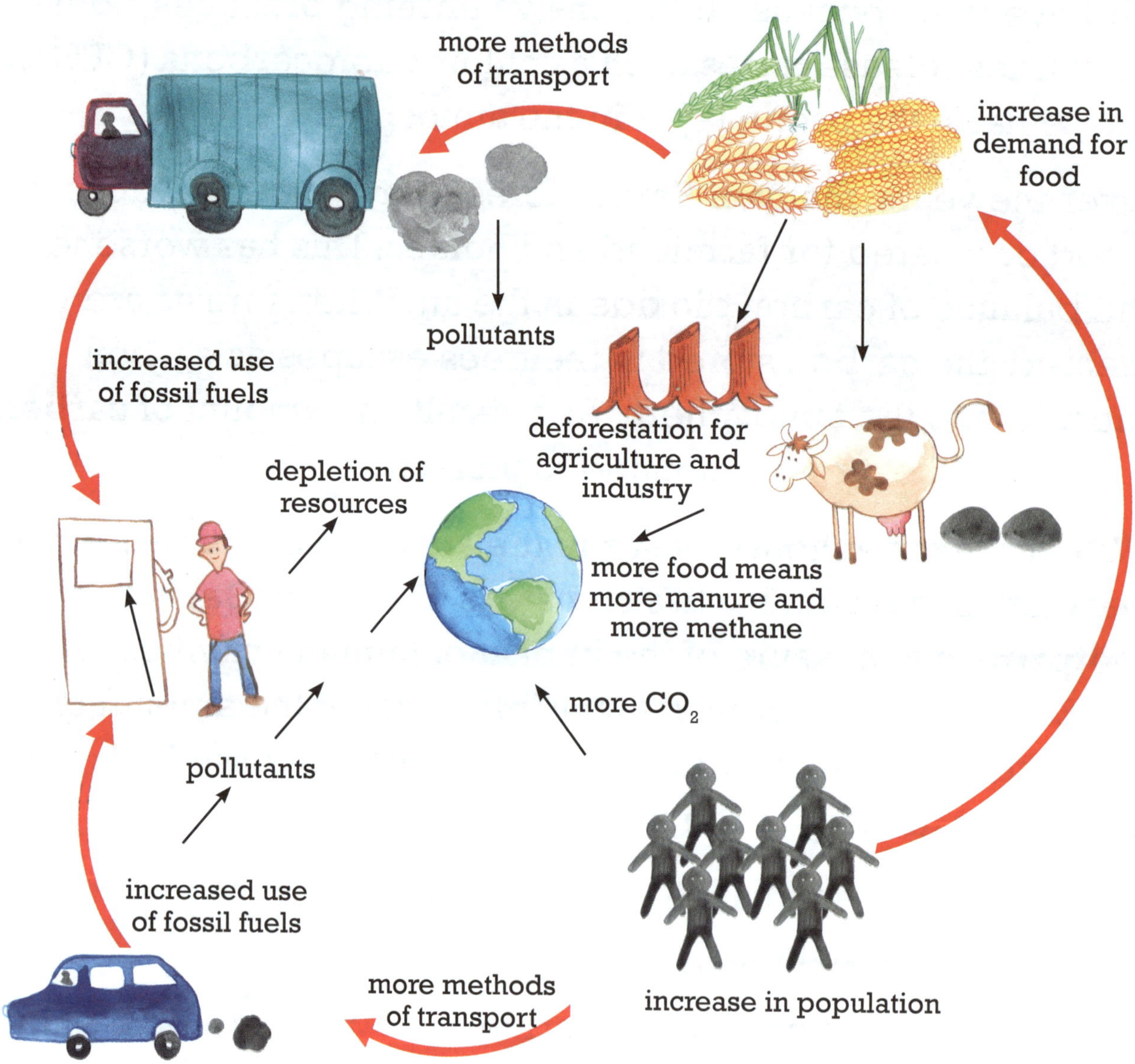

However, there are ways to save our planet from overheating. We can help in slowing down the process of global warming. Some of the things that could prove effective in the long run are listed below.

- Walking, riding your bicycle or taking the bus instead of always going by car.

 ISBN 978-81-8477-929-5

- Not wasting electricity (turning off the lights, the radio, the TV and the computer when you're not using them).
- Reducing, reusing or recycling all kinds of items, from cans to clothes, to save energy and raw materials.

- Planting more trees to help absorb excess carbon dioxide.

Explore

Divide the class into three groups. Each group will be assigned one of the following topics—water pollution, air pollution or land pollution. Each group will make a comic strip about their topic, how pollution endangers life on Earth and what measures can be taken to cut down pollution.

Quiz Time

1. Answer the questions.

a. Name the main causes of air pollution.

b. Name the main causes of water pollution.

c. Name the main causes of land pollution.

d. List some ways to reduce pollution.

e. What is climate change?

 ISBN 978-81-8477-929-5

f. Explain the greenhouse effect.

g. How does land pollution affect the environment?

2. Draw an illustration depicting the causes of global warming.

Explain the impact of climate change on our lives. How can we reduce our 'carbon footprint'?

 ISBN 978-81-8477-929-5

How to Make a Project

Science experiments and projects (and presentations) are a fantastic part of learning that allow one to engage in hands-on learning experiences. They enhance reasoning and analytical abilities as they feed the curiosity of the students.

1. **Title** – For a science project, choose a catchy title. The title could reflect on the contents of the project. It is crucial to state the essential purpose of the project.
2. **Introduction and Purpose** – This section introduces the topic of the project. It briefly explains any information already available and states the purpose of the project. State why you are interested in this topic and include citations (if any) in this section.
3. **The Hypothesis or Question** – Use this section to state your hypothesis or raise the questions that the project aims to address.
4. **Materials and Methods** – All the materials used in the project should be listed in this section. You may also describe the entire procedure used to perform the project.
5. **Data and Results** – Data refers to the actual numbers or other information obtained in the project. This information can be presented in tables or charts. The results section is where the data is used to reach the conclusion.
6. **Conclusion** – The focus of the conclusion should be to answer the question raised in the third section. Here, the data and its results should be compared and its findings should be clearly mentioned.

Alternatively, you may use the format below while starting out with a new experiment or project.

project planning	tasks	approximate number of hours
Choose a subject.		
Research information on the Internet or at the library.		
Study the information/data collected.		
Make a plan for the topic selected.		
Collect material required. (Most of the material required can be procured from around the house. Others may be easily available in retail stores.)		
Set up and perform experiments.		
Record data.		
Analyse data.		
Write a summary.		
In case of a presentation: • shop for a poster board and display materials • print out final copies of your work • put together the board presentation		
TOTAL (Add up the total estimated hours.)		

 ISBN 978-81-8477-929-5

How to Use an Encyclopedia

An encyclopedia is a useful resource found in all libraries. An encyclopedia may be a single volume, subject specific, or multi volume covering a wide range of topics. Because encyclopedias are so easy to use and so accessible, many people use encyclopedias as their first option for a reference tool.

Most general encyclopedias are multivolume sets and are set up in alphabetical format. Some encyclopedias may need you to know the key word or subject heading in order to find specific information covered over a variety of volumes. Some encyclopedias devote separate volumes to different subjects.

Locate the index. The index is usually in the last series of volumes and is in alphabetical order. It gives you page numbers and volume numbers to locate the article you are researching.

Read the article and pick out relevant information for your project.

For teachers

A. Pass a volume of an encyclopedia to a group of students. Ask them to go through the layout, the way the information is organised and the quickest way to locate an entry. Challenge each group to compile an encyclopedia on any topic. Topics could be children's authors, unique inventions, historical sites in Asia, etc.

B. Ask the students to read an entry on any animal of their choice. Encourage the students to write a newspaper article or a poem using all the details and facts from the entry.

Pink is my nose

I thrive on garbage

Go away, my friend

Tips

- Look out for other cross-references that can broaden your topic and provide new insight into your research.
- Pay attention to the maps, graphs and pictures in the article.
- The outline, provided for longer articles, is a helpful reference tool when organising your writing.
- Refer to authors correctly. The information on authors is either in the introductory material or in the index.

B

*BAHAMAS see *CARIBBEAN SEA & ISLANDS
*BAHRAIN see *MIDDLE EAST

*BALKANS
The Balkan Peninsula extends into the western end of the Mediterranean Sea. The region has a long history of political and religious division.

KEY FACTS
AREA 200,000 sq. mi. (518,000 sq. km)
POPULATION 50,000,000
COUNTRIES 9
LARGEST COUNTRY Romania
SMALLEST COUNTRY Slovenia
RELIGIONS Islam, Orthodox, Roman Catholicism
LANGUAGES Albanian, Bosnian, Bulgarian, Croatian, Macedonian, Romanian, Serbian, Slovenian, Turkish

The Balkan states include the countries of Albania, Bulgaria, Greece, and Romania, plus the countries that once made up Yugoslavia: Croatia, Macedonia, Bosnia and Herzegovina, Slovenia, and the new confederation (partnership) of Serbia and Montenegro.

Land and climate
This is a mountainous region: Down the coast of Croatia, Yugoslavia, and Albania strings of mountains, an extension of the European Alps, form an impressive barrier that drops down to the shore of the Adriatic Sea.

Look in the Index for: *BACH, JOHANN SEBASTIAN *BALBOA, VASCO NÚÑEZ DE

50

 ISBN 978-81-8477-929-5

How to Use the Internet

One of the most recent and popular resource for research is the Internet. The Internet is a repository of information collected from various sources. Navigating through sites and links can give you updated information. Though the Internet is a wealth of information, before proceeding on any topic, take an adult's help to determine which sites might be reliable and which might not be a good source.

Tips

- It is a good idea to sit with an adult and bookmark the sites that you will need for research. This way you can directly go to the pages you want to view.
- Before beginning the topic, write down some keywords on which you will base your research.
- Use quality, child-friendly search engines such as www.ajkids.com (Ask Jeeves Kids) and www.yahooligans.com (Yahooligans!). You can keep a list of helpful sites near the computer for easy access.
- Quotation marks are important while conducting a topic search. If you enter your topic or key words without quotation marks around it, the search will give information about anything linked to the words. If you put the search topic in quotation marks, you will get information related to the exact words placed within quotation marks.
- If you can't read through the entire article, you can use the FIND option to locate a particular word in the article.

For teachers

Divide the class into four groups. Give three groups a topic to research and present. These groups will have different resources to research. The fourth group will then review the depth and breadth of the information, and survey and compare all the sources. They can present their report based on:

Which source gave you more information?

Which source gave you better information?

 ISBN 978-81-8477-929-5